The Perigal and Duterrau
watch and clockmakers

The Perigal and Duterrau watch and clockmakers

PERIGAL & DUTERRAU WATCH AND
CLOCKMAKERS TO THE KING

Nicolette Reichhold

Copyright © 2015 Nicolette Reichhold
All rights reserved.

First Printing: 2015

ISBN: 1514787172
ISBN 13: 9781514787175

nheesom@hotmail.co.uk

Acknowledgements

I would like to thank Emma Reichhold for her help with this manuscript, Stephen Aris for the photograph on the cover and Jeffrey Lehrer for setting out the genealogical tables. Many thanks also to the following people: David Penney for information on the watches made by the Perigal and Duterrau families, Roger Smith for confirming the Swiss origin of the Duterrau family, Jean Wood, Sally Goodsir of the Royal Collection Trust, the archivist at Winchester College, Hampshire and the helpful staff at the Guildhall library.

Lastly, I would like to thank the following who gave me permission to use their pictures: David Penney, Jean Wood, the Guildhall library and The National Trust.

Contents

	Introduction ix
	Genealogical tree of the Perigal family xii
	Genealogical tree of the Duterrau family xiii
Chapter 1	The Perigal watch and clockmakers 1
Chapter 2	Claude Perigal (1 & 2) of Rose Street, Soho 3
Chapter 3	Francis Perigal (1, 2 & 3) of the Royal Exchange 5
Chapter 4	Watch production at 9, Royal Exchange 7
Chapter 5	Clock production at 9, Royal Exchange 10
Chapter 6	John Perigal of Coventry Street 13
Chapter 7	Francis Perigal (4) of Bond Street before Perigal & Duterrau 16
Chapter 8	Watch production at Bond Street before Perigal & Duterrau 19
Chapter 9	Clock production at Bond Street before Perigal & Duterrau 23
Chapter 10	Markwick, Markham and Perigal 26
Chapter 11	The Duterrau family of Rose Street, Soho 28
Chapter 12	The first generation of Duterrau watchmakers 30
Chapter 13	The second generation: the 3 sons of James Duterrau (1) 33
Chapter 14	The third and fourth generation of Duterrau watchmakers 37
Chapter 15	Perigal & Duterrau of New Bond Street and Poland Street 40

Chapter 16 Perigal & Duterrau: watch production · · · · · · · · · · · · · · · · · 47
Chapter 17 Perigal & Duterrau: clock production · · · · · · · · · · · · · · · · · 51
Chapter 18 The last years of Perigal & Duterrau · · · · · · · · · · · · · · · · · · · 55
        Appendix A: The Francis Perigal Watch and Clockmakers 57
        Appendix B: Twenty-Two Perigal & Duterrau Watches · · · 59
        Appendix C: Perigal & Duterrau in
        Thwaites Daybook (1800) · 61
        Bibliography · 63
        Glossary · 65
        Abbreviations Used in Endnotes · 66
        Endnotes · 67

Introduction

THE PERIGAL FAMILY WAS FAMOUS for their high-quality watches and clocks in 18th and 19th century London, owning several prestigious firms. One distinguished member of the family was a Francis Perigal who had a shop in New Bond Street and a Royal Appointment as a watchmaker in ordinary to King George III. Sometime in the late 1790s, having reached his fifties, he took his brother-in-law John Duterrau into partnership and the firm of Perigal and Duterrau began. It remained a family firm throughout its existence, as after the deaths of Francis and John, it was taken over by John's son, John (2), who was known as John Francis Duterrau. He was left in sole charge of the firm until about 1845, when he sold it to a competitor in New Bond Street. I have a particular interest in this firm as my grandmother's grandmother, born Matilda Sarah Duterrau at 62, New Bond Street in 1815, was one of the four children of John Francis Duterrau.

The first chapter of this book looks at the biographical background of the early Perigal watch and clockmakers and the relationships between them, though not all of them can be fitted into the Perigal family tree. Subsequent chapters describe some of the firms owned by the Perigals, with chapter ten looking at the Perigal involvement with the firm of Markham, Markwick and Perigal, maker of clocks and watches for the Ottoman market. The fact that several of the Perigal watch and clockmakers had the first name of Francis has led to much confusion. In particular, Francis Perigal of New Bond Street has often been mixed up or conflated with one or other of the three Francis Perigals who worked at the Royal

Exchange. As a result, advertisements for auctions and sales of a Francis Perigal clock or watch are often accompanied by inaccurate biographical details. Appendix A has a summary of the various Francis Perigals.

Much less is known about the Duterrau watch and clock makers, the descendants of a migrant from Fribourg in Switzerland who had arrived in London early in the 18th century. Chapters 11-14 describes the six Duterrau watch and clock makers. There is also the story of an apprentice watchmaker called Thomas Duterrau, who made an unsuccessful attempt to set up a branch of Perigal and Duterrau in Australia in 1835. Several connections between the two families can be found, starting from the 1720s, when members of the Perigal and Duterrau families rented property in the same street in Soho. This was followed by an apprenticeship of a Duterrau to a Perigal in 1730, the links continuing with two marriages. The culmination of this relationship was the formation of the firm of Perigal and Duterrau in New Bond Street, which is the subject of the last four chapters. Though I am not a horologist, I have looked at the watch and clock production of all the firms mentioned in this book, concentrating particularly on Francis Perigal of New Bond Street (circa 1770 to the late1790s) and of Perigal and Duterrau, the firm that he founded.

An important source for the genealogy of the Perigal family is a book called *Some Account of the Perigal Family*, published in 1887 by Frederick Perigal, a grandson of the second of the three Francis Perigals of the Royal Exchange.[1] The original version of this book has a genealogical tree including dates, which have been checked by his many descendants, as well as by others, and found to be accurate. All the dates and relationships in the genealogical tree of the Perigal watchmakers which follows are identical to those found in Frederick Perigal's book, the information in the Duterrau genealogical tree coming from a variety of sources. In order to make the trees clearer, I have omitted those members of the family who were not watch and clock makers unless they were needed for genealogical purposes.

A variety of other sources were used for this book. Most of the details of the births, marriages and deaths came from the usual sources in ancestry.co.uk and findmypast.co.uk. Huguenot records were also used, as both the families attended Huguenot Chapels. Additional biographical information came from sources such as the Sun Fire Insurance policies at the London Metropolitan Archives and the more specialised records in the family history websites, for example, the Westminster rate books in findmypast.co.uk and the Freedom of the City Admission papers in ancestry.co.uk. The Duterrau surname appears in many variants in these records, the most common being Duterran and Duter(r)eau.

Information about the clock and watchmaking activities of the two families was obtained from sources such as the standard horological textbooks of Britten, Baillie and Brian Loomes, apprenticeship records and trade directories. A useful source for the three Perigals of the Royal Exchange was the online site of *The Worshipful Company of Clockmakers* (the pages on 'Clockmasters and their Apprentices' and 'Masters since 1631'). The online *Database of Court Officers 1660-1837* indexed by R. O. Bucholz has some information on Royal appointments, with further details to be found in the National Archives at Kew. Amongst the sources used from the clock library at London's Guildhall were the daybooks of the trade manufacturer Thwaites & Reed, as well as several books on clocks, watches and their makers. Another useful source was the journal of The Antiquarian Horological Society.[75] Some of the terms used are defined in a glossary.

The descendants of the Duterrau family have retained a few mementoes of their watchmaking ancestors, for example, my third cousin Jean Wood owns the ring gauges once used in the shop in New Bond Street, as well as some of the personal financial records of John Duterrau (1) and his son, John Francis Duterrau (2). Two photographic versions of a portrait of John Francis Duterrau are still in existence, though the whereabouts of the original is unknown. The family also has a few stories about the Duterrau watchmakers.

Nicolette Reichhold

Genealogical tree of the Perigal family

(watch/clockmakers in bold)

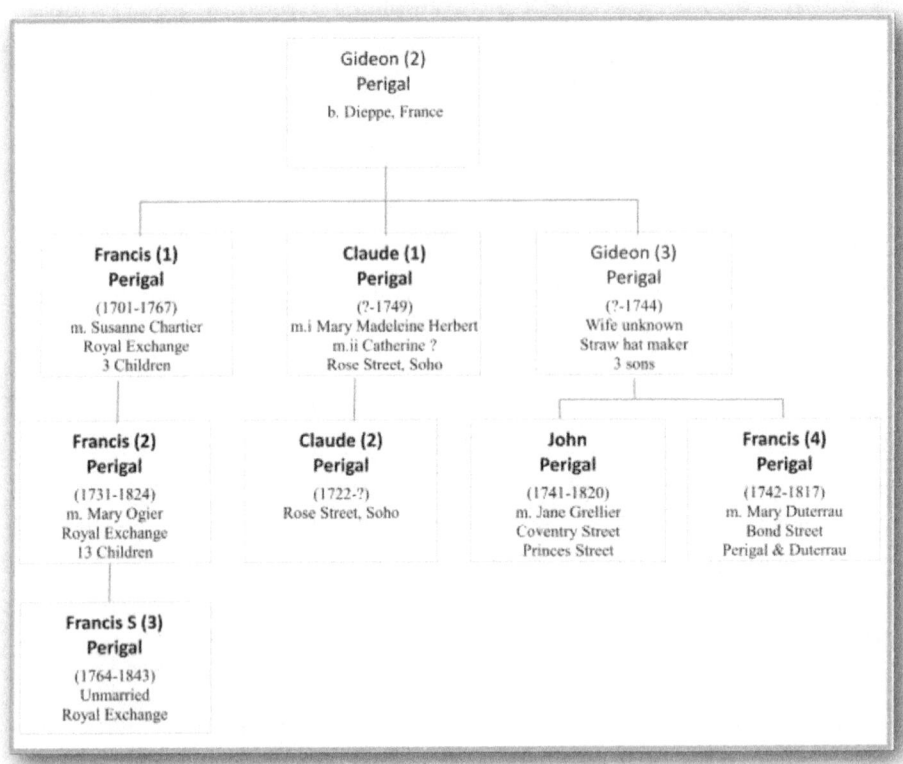

Correction: Francis Perigal (2) was born in 1734

Genealogical tree of the Duterrau family

(watch/clockmakers in bold)

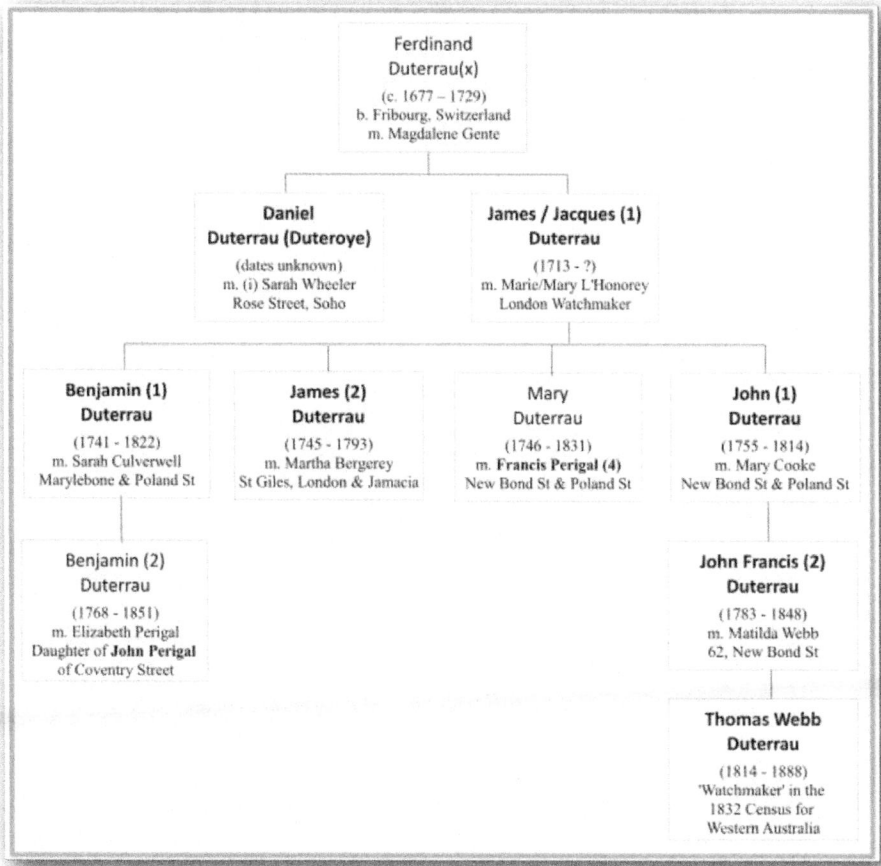

CHAPTER 1

The Perigal watch and clockmakers

ON 27 APRIL 1688, AFTER much persecution, the Huguenot refugees, Gideon Perigal (1), his wife Magdalene and their son Jean were released from prison in Dieppe and allowed to travel to London. There they were reunited with their sons, Gideon (2) and Jacques and their daughter Marthe, who had made their escape separately (Frederick Perigal p.28). Several watch and clockmakers with the surname Perigal can be found in 18th and 19th century London, all of whom are thought to be descendants of Gideon Perigal (1).

Frederick Perigal concentrates mainly on his own particular branch of the Perigals, the descendants of Gideon Perigal (2), but records reveal that there were further London watch and clock makers who are not mentioned in his book. One of these was another Gideon Perigal: on 10 July 1718 an 'Elizabeth Perigall, wife of Gideon Perigall of Clerkenwell Green in the County of Middx Watchmaker' was a witness at the City of London Sessions.[2] Perhaps this is the same man who is listed by Baillie as the maker of a watch in a jasper case, working in London in 1710, as well as the Gideon Perigal who took on an apprentice called Thomas Player in 1710 (Britten). Another Perigal of unknown parentage was a 'Mr. Perigal watchmaker Shandois Street, Isaac Carter his apprentice'. Apparently he did not do well, as he can be found in the St. Martin in the Fields Poor Law records for 1736.[3] A Thomas Perigal, listed as working in Coventry

1

Street in 1784 was more successful.[4] Thomas may have been working for John Perigal, who had a watchmaking business at 11-12 Coventry Street at the time, but the exact relationship between them is unknown. There are also further Francis Perigals who cannot be fitted into the Perigal family tree (see Appendix A).

In his account of his family, Frederick Perigal provides some information on each of the watchmakers, including their places of work. He describes one of the brothers of Francis Perigal (1) as a Claude Perigal of Rose Street who died in 1749, but does not mention his occupation. It is apparent, however, that Claude was in fact a watchmaker of some repute (see next chapter). All the clock and watchmaking descendants of Gideon Perigal (2) turned out to be successful, owning highly reputable firms, a list made by the King's clockmaker, Benjamin Vulliamy in 1782, naming the three clock and watchmaking firms owned by the Perigal family in that year as follows: [5]

Perigal .... *Bond Street*
Perigal .... *Exchange*
Perigal .... *Coventry Street*

It is apparent from the genealogical tree that the owners of these firms were closely related, the Francis Perigal (1) who had founded the business at the Royal Exchange being the uncle of both Francis (4) of Bond Street and John of Coventry Street.

CHAPTER 2

Claude Perigal (1 &2) of Rose Street, Soho

Claude Perigal (1) appears in Baillie as follows:

Perigal, Claude (1), London (Rose Street) d.1749 'One of the most eminent men in England for making motions for rep. Watches'

APPRENTICE RECORDS SHOW THAT CLAUDE took on two apprentices, Stephen La Vigne in 1734 and Richard Willder in 1742.[6] One of Claude's watches, a repeater with gold poker and beetle hands numbered 1749, was recently sold at auction.[7] In 1745 his brother, Francis Perigal (1) 'Watchmaker, the North Side of the Royal Exchange' offered a reward of eight guineas for the return of a repeating silver watch numbered 2120 that had been made by Claude.[8] The watch had been 'Lost, mislaid, pawn'd or left in the Hands of some unknown person, by a Gentleman that was killed at the Battle of Fontenoy'.

Claude's first wife was Mary Magdelaine, the daughter of Antoine Hébert, a watchmaker in Horse Shoe Alley, Shoreditch (Frederick Perigal p.35). Their son Claude (2) was born on 25 November 1722 and baptised at the Huguenot Chapel at Hungerford Market, with his grandfather as his godfather.[9] Claude (1) died intestate, Frederick Perigal noting that Claude's second wife, Catherine was 'Executrix to her husband Adm 4 Jan 1750'. This refers to a document revealing the existence of stock to the value of £250 held in the joint names of Stephen Goujon, Claude Perigal and Louis Blanck.[10] The Stephen Goujon in this document was probably the man who made elaborate watch-cases for the Perigals of the Royal Exchange (see later). Claude (2) was another watchmaker, a 1751 Westminster rate book entry for 'Claudius Perigall' at a house in Rose Street indicating that he had taken over his father's business.[11]

CHAPTER 3

Francis Perigal (1, 2 & 3) of the Royal Exchange

FRANCIS PERIGAL (1) (1701-1767), THE founder of the business at the Royal Exchange, was born in 1701 to Gideon, a goldsmith at the sign of the Cross Keys in St. Martin's Lane and his wife, Janne Du Coudre.[12] He was apprenticed to a goldsmith called Henry Duck in 1715 for a fee of £10.[13] On 24 August 1726, he married Susanne Chartier at the French Huguenot Chapel in Castle Street, their son Francis (2) being born in 1734.[14] During the time that he worked in St Martin in the Fields, Francis had two apprentices; firstly James Duterrau, the son of 'Magdelaine', a widow from St Martin in the Fields for a fee of £10 in 1730.[15] The second apprentice, a Peter Goay, son of a weaver from Spitalfields, was taken on for £20 in 1737.[16] On 21 October 1740, at the age of 39, Francis gained the Freedom of the City of London by the payment of the sum of 46 shillings and 8 pence.[17] After his arrival in the City he had at least two further apprentices, his son Francis (2) in 1748 and a Christopher Beck in 1752.[18]

In Kent's Directory for 1753 Francis's Perigal's address is given as 'behind the Exchange, Threadneedle-street, London', subsequent directories placing him and/or his descendants at '9, Threadneedle street London' (Kent's 1768) and 'No. 9 North Piazza, Royal Exchange, London' (Andrews New London Directory for 1789). Francis's clock and watchmaking business was passed successively to his son and grandson, each of them being named Francis, records showing that Francis Perigal (3) was apprenticed to his father on 6 July 1778.[19] This was a large and highly prestigious business, with each of the three Francis Perigals in turn achieving the distinguished role of Master of the Clockmakers Company, Francis (1) in 1756, Francis (2) in 1775 and Francis (3) (who is described in the record as 'Francis S. Perigal Jnr.') in 1806.[20] Francis Perigal (1) died in Twickenham in 1767, leaving the business to his son Francis (2).[21] By the 1790s Francis (2) appears in some directories together with his son as Francis Perigal Senior and Junior and from 1793 onwards as 'Messrs Perigal & Son' or 'Messrs Perigal' in the daybooks of Thwaites and Reed.[22] This father and son partnership did not have any connection with the business at New Bond Street, nor did they receive any Royal appointments, though they have frequently been credited with both. The business at the Royal Exchange was to last for about 100 years, finally coming to an end in 1843, with the death of Francis S. Perigal (3), the grandson of the founder: his father Francis (2) had died in 1824.[23]

CHAPTER 4

Watch production at 9, Royal Exchange

FRANCIS PERIGAL (2) AND (3) of the Royal Exchange give their professions as 'Watchmaker' in directories, though this does not necessarily mean that they produced watches on their premises. With some exceptions the firm used a five digit production number for their watches. From the five digit numbers of three of their watches, together with the hallmarks of their original cases, it is possible to estimate that during the period from 1774 to 1791 the firm was producing an average of over two hundred watches annually.[24] This was a high rate of production, a more typical number for a quality firm, for example that of Josiah Emery, being in the region of forty watches a year.[25]

A description and picture of a quarter-repeating watch, with a diamond endstone signed 'Francis Perigal London' numbered 13818 gives an idea of the luxurious and no doubt expensive watches sold by The Perigals of the Royal Exchange.[26] The outer case, made by Stephen Goujon, Master of the Clockmakers Company is of agate overlaid with embossed flowers and scrolls studded with diamonds, emeralds, rubies and a sapphire in a gold setting. As it is dated circa 1760 it could have been made by either Francis Perigal (1) or (2): Francis (2) had been freed from his apprenticeship on 5 April 1756. A repeating watch engraved 'Perigal London' dated 1760-5 and numbered 915 has (according to a recent seller) several similarities to this one, though it does not have the gem and diamond setting.[27] The case of this watch is made by Daniel Aveline, (a former apprentice of Stephen Goujon), who is known to have made cases for the Royal Exchange Perigals.[28] It is likely that this watch was made at the Royal Exchange, but the reasons why it was not given a five digit number are unclear.

It is apparent from a watch in the Victoria and Albert Museum that the Royal Exchange Perigals also commissioned the services of Stephen Goujon's son, the casemaker, Peter Goujon. This watch was made by Francis (2) as it is numbered 15754 and dated to circa 1770 (Francis (1) had died in 1767). The Metropolitan Museum of Art in New York has two further examples of watches made by the Perigals of the Royal Exchange. One of these, a repeater watch, numbered 17389 with 'Perigal Royal Exchange London' on the dial, has hands that are 'richly set with small diamonds', the Turkish numerals showing that the watch had been designed for export to the Ottoman market.[29] The Fitzwilliam Museum in Cambridge also has one of their watches.

In the Ashmolean Museum in Oxford there is a gold pair-cased quarter-repeating watch dated by the museum to before 1770, which is signed 'Perigal LONDON 1465'on the movement. There is an inner case made by Daniel Aveline and an outer dust cap inscribed 'Jno Perigal 1465'. The museum believe that this cap is a later addition to an earlier watch and attribute the watch to one of the Perigals of the Royal Exchange, mainly on the basis that John was not in business as a watchmaker until 1770. John had been freed from his apprenticeship in 1762, however, so it is possible that he had had a more active role in the making of this watch, either by himself or in collusion with his close relatives at the Royal Exchange (Francis Perigal (2) was his first-cousin). It is apparent that John made watches with similarities to this one, for example, a pair-cased quarter-repeating watch numbered 1430 which has been attributed to John Perigal has the same arcaded minutes noted as an unusual feature of the watch in the Ashmolean Museum.[30] According to David Penney, John also made use of the case-maker Daniel Aveline.

There are several watches with signatures varying from 'Fras. Perigal', 'F. Perigal', 'Perigal London', 'Perigal' and 'Perigal junior' which do not have any indication as to who made them. It is very likely that some of them came from Royal Exchange, for example, the watches signed 'Perigal junior' could have been made by Francis (3): there is a watch signed 'Perigal junior', numbered 1397.[31] John Perigal of Coventry Street and his brother Francis (4) of New Bond Street were probably also responsible for some of these watches. At the end of the 18th century, London watchmakers were famous all over Europe, so it became a common practice among some foreign watchmakers to attempt to push up the prices of their watches by copying the styles and forging the signatures of well-known London watchmakers. It is highly likely, therefore, that some of the watches with the Perigal signature are fakes.

CHAPTER 5

Clock production at 9, Royal Exchange

CLOCKS MADE BY THE PERIGALS of the Royal Exchange turn up fairly frequently at auctions. If these clocks are typical of their overall output, it looks as if the Perigals were particularly fond of musical clocks. There is a picture of one of them, a musical bracket clock with four tunes, in a book by Marie de Gallier Sander.[32] Like many other clock and watchmakers of the time, they used the services of the well-known trade manufacturer John Thwaites, from the firm that later became Thwaites & Reed. This company supplied everything from parts of clocks to movements, as well as complete clocks made to their customer's specification, with many of the famous clockmaking families of the time, such as the Ellicotts and the Vulliamys, using their services. Entries in the daybooks of Thwaites & Reed show that 'Messrs Perigal' or 'Messrs Perigal & Son' placed a variety of orders, ranging from complete new clocks and parts of clocks to repair and maintenance jobs.[33] In September 1794, for example, they asked for '2 New Musical Clocks to play every 3 hours' and in January 1805 for some regulators which were to be made 'in the best manner'. Thwaites's movements are often found in clocks made for the Ottoman and Chinese markets, so it is likely that they were in at least some of the clocks that the Perigals exported (see below).

Exotic clocks designed specifically for the Ottoman market by the Perigals of the Royal Exchange can occasionally be found at auctions. One of them is an early George III veneered tortoiseshell musical bracket clock with a dome-shaped case (the shape of a mosque) with Turkish numerals, signed 'Francis Perigal Royal Exchange': musical clocks were particularly in favour in Turkey at this time.[34] A 'Francis Perigal' is listed in a catalogue of the clocks and watches in the Topkapi Sarayi Museum in Istanbul, compiled circa 1966.[35] As there is no evidence that Francis Perigal (4) of Bond Street made clocks or watches for export to the Ottoman Empire it is very probable that this entry referred to one of the Francis Perigals from the Royal Exchange.

In the second half of the 18th century, many London clockmakers made elaborate musical clocks with automata for export to China by the East Indian Company. Known as the 'sing-song' trade, these clocks were mainly bought as official presents to rulers, but were also widely used by ship's officers as bribes to local officials and merchants.[36] A list of the sixty-nine London clock and watchmakers whose work could be found in the Palace Museum at Peking (Beijing) includes the name of Francis Perigal.[37] While cataloguing these clocks in the Beijing Palace Museum in the 1930s, Simon Harcourt-Smith found that:[38]

The passage of hours was marked by the fluttering of enamelled wings, and a gushing of glass fountains, and a spinning of paste stars, while from a thousand concealed and whirring orchestras the Gavottes and Minuets of London rose strangely into the Chinese air

Recently, Sotheby's sold a musical automaton table clock, made by a Francis Perigal from the Royal Exchange circa 1790, which was formerly in the court of the Emperor Qian Long (1736-96). The clock, which had been acquired by the Swiss watch importer, Gustave Loup (1876-1961) from the Imperial Palace at Jehol, has a three train fusee movement and verge escapement and various automata.[39] These include two separate moving ships encircling revolving glass waterfall rods in the cupola, whilst elsewhere in the clock flying birds circle in a rural scene, the action being accompanied by one of four different tunes. In the June 2015 edition of

Antiquarian Horology there are four views of this clock, one of which (some detail from the country scene in the break arch) is also pictured on the cover.[40]

There was at least one further clock made by the Perigals of the Royal Exchange in a Chinese Imperial court as, according to Sotheby's, there is a Francis Perigal elephant clock dated 1775 currently in the Beijing Palace Museum.[41] This is a version of a clock made by a Peter Torckler consisting mostly of a large ormolu elephant with articulated trunk, ears and tail which move in conjunction with a choice of tunes. The relatively small size of the clock dial indicates that the time-keeping properties were seen as almost an irrelevance. Another of their clocks, an ormolu musical quarter-striking table clock sold at an auction in 2004, had obviously been designed to appeal to the Chinese market.[42] The case of the clock is surmounted by a pagoda, a placard with Chinese characters rising within the case whenever the clock strikes the quarter. Broadly translated, the characters on the placard read as follows: 'May you have five sons who pass sufficient exams and become high officers in Government'.

CHAPTER 6

John Perigal of Coventry Street

FREDERICK PERIGAL'S BOOK HAS THE following comment on John: 'John was a silversmith in Coventry Street, in partnership with Lewis Masquerier ..' (p.37). John Perigal, the elder brother of Francis Perigal of Bond Street, was born on 28 January 1741.[43] At the age of fourteen, he was apprenticed to Henry Long, a watchmaker from St. Giles in the Field, for an apprenticeship fee of £50.[44] By 1773, John and his partner Lewis Masquerier were trading from the 'Ring & Pearl' at 11, Coventry Street, where they had been licensed to sell a 'Mock Oriental Pearl' patented by a Samuel Archer of Goswell Street.[45] A trade card for Masquerier and Perigal at the Ring & Pearl describes their business as follows:[46]

> *Make and Sell Variety of Plate, Jewells (sic), Watches & Toys in the most Elegant Taste. Likewise Great Variety of Plated Goods, Hardware and Cutlery. The full Value given for Second-hand Plate, Jewells and Watches*

('Toys' were small items, such as jewellery, snuff boxes, scent bottles and decorated watch cases, all of which sold well at the time.)

In 1777 the firm ran into financial trouble, the partners being declared bankrupt.[47] They were allowed to continue trading, however, as in January 1778, Masquerier & Perigal of 12, Coventry Street took out an insurance policy for £1,000, which values their stock for £850.[48] Afraid of losing their customers, the partners placed an advertisement in a newspaper to ask for the 'continuation of the favours of the nobility and others', the advertisement ending with the following sales pitch:[49]

> *N.B. Hair Bracelets, Watch and Cane Hair Strings, Arms, Cyphers & with every other device that can possibly be done in hair are executed in their shop, in the utmost perfection (and with great care that the hair given is not changed)*

In spite of the bankruptcy proceedings, the firm of Masquerier & Perigal appears to have been a success, as according to Britten, the partners were appointed as goldsmiths and jewellers to the Duke of York.

By the late 18th century the jurisdiction of the Clockmakers Company did not extend beyond the square mile of the City of London, so the Company decided to admit a number of people practising in London independently of the Company to the rank of Honorary Freemen. These gentlemen would be 'men whose practical knowledge of the Art would be valuable in the protection of rights and privileges of the Craft and whose social position would enable them to render useful service in defence of its interests'.[50] On 2 July 1781, both John and his brother Francis (4) became part of this select group, indicating that they were seen as respected figures in the clock and watchmaking community.

The partnership of Masquerier & Perigal was dissolved in 1782, with John continuing to 'carry out the trade of Watch and Clock Maker in Coventry St', while his partner took over the goldsmith and jewellery side of the business.[51] An advertisement in 1784 for a lost watch gives an idea of the sort of watches made by John: it was a gold stopwatch, horizontal, capped and jewelled, engraved 'John Perigal London 1944', with an enamelled woman's head.[52] Another partnership, this time with Renock Browne (the firm called Perigal & Browne, clock and watchmakers), was dissolved in 1799, the *London Gazette* for June 1799 announcing that any person indebted to this firm should contact 'Mr. John Perigal, No 12 Coventry –Street, where the business will be carried out as usual'.[53] Kent's directory for 1794 lists the firm of Perigal & Browne at 11,

Coventry Street, with John Perigal at number 12. A picture of a chronometer watch, made by the firm of Perigal and Browne can be found in the catalogue of the British Museum.[54]

Near the beginning of the 19th century, John moved to 55, Princes Street, Soho, where in 1808 he gives his occupation as 'watchmaker and goldsmith' (*Kelly's Post Office Annual Directory* for 1808). By 1803, Francis Lambert, a goldsmith, silversmith and jeweller had set up shop in John's former premises at 11 and 12 Coventry Street.[55] A picture of the Georgian shop front of Lambert and Rawlings at 10-12 Coventry Street can be found in *John Tallis's London Street Views*.[56] These pictures were drawn between 1838 and 1840, however, so it is possible that the buildings had changed since John worked there.

John's bankruptcy problems were solved in 1797, when a final settlement was made with the bankruptcy court.[57] Later, he appears to have made a good living, as in 1810 his daughter Elizabeth insures a house at 2, Great Pulteney Street.[58] This was most probably her dowry from her father, as in 1812, Elizabeth's new husband Benjamin Duterrau (2) insures the same house for the sum of £700.[59] John Perigal retired to Hammersmith, where he died aged 79, on 3 June 1820.[60]

CHAPTER 7

Francis Perigal (4) of Bond Street before Perigal & Duterrau

FREDERICK PERIGAL COMMENTS ON FRANCIS Perigal (4) as follows: 'Francis was a Watchmaker in Bond Street and Poland Street, in partnership with Duterreau whose sister he married. He and his wife were buried in Hammersmith Churchyard' (p.37). The younger brother of John of Coventry Street, Francis was born in 1742.[61] On 15 August 1765 he married Mary Duterrau at the Church of St. Martin in the Fields.[62] Mary (or Marie) came from a watchmaking family, her three brothers were all watchmakers and her father James had been an apprentice of Francis Perigal (1), the founder of the clock and watchmaking business at 9, Royal Exchange. Both the Perigals and the Duterraus attended the wedding: one of the witnesses was 'Fra Perigal' the other was Mary's father James. According to the marriage transcript, Francis came from the parish of St. Giles. Probably he was the 'Frans Perigal of St Giles in the Fields Watchmkr' who took on an apprentice called James Abraham Goldwin for a fee of £30 in 1765.[63] There are two further apprenticeship records in which a watchmaker called Francis Perigal, (one of St Anne Soho in 1767, the other of Rathbone Place in 1770) acquired an apprentice, which could refer to Francis Perigal (4) before his arrival in Bond Street (see Appendix A).

By the 1770s Francis had started trading from Bond Street, a Westminster Rate Book assessment showing that in 1779 he was renting

16

property in both Old and New Bond Street.[64] In the same year he insured a property and its contents at 57, New Bond Street for £700.[65] Nearby Hanover Square was a popular address for aristocrats at the time, with Bond Street serving as 'a fashionable promenade for the *beau monde* very quickly becoming famous as a luxury shopping street', so he had chosen an excellent place to set up his business.[66] In 1791 he acquired an apprentice called Solomon Smith, for the relatively high apprenticeship fee of £63.[67]

It is apparent that Francis's career as a watchmaker in New Bond Street was a distinguished one. He became an Honorary Freeman of the Clockmakers Company in 1781 and just three years later on the first of January 1784, the newly appointed Lord Chamberlain, Lord Salisbury, issued a Royal Warrant on behalf of King George III, requesting that 'Mr. Francis Perigal' be sworn in as :

> *One of the Watchmakers in Ordinary to His Majesty ... to have hold exercise and enjoy the said place together with all Rights Profits Privileges and Advantages thereunto belonging*

This appointment would have brought him considerable prestige. From this time onwards his watches were engraved with the words 'Watchmaker to his Majesty', while his directory entries show him as 'watch maker to the King'.[68] The chief Royal watchmaker at this time, as shown by the *Royal Kalendar*, was Thomas Mudge, the most celebrated watchmaker of his time. Due to ill-health, Thomas Mudge rarely came to London, so it is possible that Francis Perigal carried out Mudge's Royal duties as a proxy. A Royal Warrant in the quarter from 5 April to 5 July 1794, in which 'Perigal Fras Clock Maker' was paid six guineas, shows that he did at least some work in the Royal palaces, though unfortunately the work that he had carried out for his Royal client is not divulged.[69] Francis Perigal's Royal Appointment would also have helped him financially: he would have received the annual salary of £150 given to Royal Tradesmen and would have been able to charge higher prices for his clocks and watches, but bankruptcy would have meant instant dismissal from his post.[70] In addition to this, Francis has been described by Cecil Clutton as 'one of the pioneers of the lever escapement'.[71]

The identities of some of Francis Perigal (4)'s customers between 1784 and 1798 are revealed in the daybooks of the trade manufacturer Thwaites & Reed.[72] In 1788, for example, Francis Perigal subcontracted work on a turret clock belonging to a Lord Talbot, with a similar job taking place on his behalf in the same year for a Bond Hopkins Esq. at an address near Cobham. The following year Francis gave Thwaites two further commissions, one on behalf of Lord Fairford at Hertford Castle and the other for Lord Melbourne. Later clients of Francis Perigal include a Mr. Franklin in 1794, Samuel Whitbread Junior Esq. (1795) and a Sir Horace Mann from Eggerton in Kent in the same year. His most frequent customer during this period, with six commissions, was Lord Salisbury of Hatfield House.[73] This was probably James Cecil, the first Marquess of Salisbury, appointed Lord Chancellor of the Household in 1784, who had signed the warrant for Francis Perigal's appointment as a watchmaker to King George III. Given Francis Perigal's Royal duties it seems very likely that the two men were acquainted.

CHAPTER 8

Watch production at Bond Street before Perigal & Duterrau

WATCHES MADE BY FRANCIS PERIGAL of Bond Street, with their three and four digit production numbers, can usually be distinguished from those of the Perigals of the Royal Exchange, who mostly used five digit numbers. In addition, all of the five watches in the list below are engraved with 'Bond Street' and/or 'Watchmaker to his Majesty'.

Five of the watches made by Francis Perigal (4) of New Bond Street [74]

Production number	Date	Type of watch	
392	1780	Verge escapement & fusee, gold pair cases	1
460	ca1781-2	Cylinder, regulator dial, silver case	2
708	1786	Cylinder, seconds stop watch, gold case	3
1053	after 1787	Perigal's early lever escapement watch	4
1189	after 1787	Verge escapement & fusee	5

Watch 1 has the original pair cases, with the London hallmark for 1780 and a case-maker's mark for IW. The motion is signed 'Fra Perigal Bond

Street 392'. As watch 3 also has its original cases, it is possible to estimate that Francis's Bond Street business was producing of the order of sixty-five watches a year between 1780 and 1786. This is less than half the number of watches produced by the Perigals of the Royal Exchange in a similar time period.

Watch 2 is signed 'Fra Perigal, Bond Street, London, no 460', the number indicating that the watch was made in about 1781-2. The case, which has the case-maker's mark for Daniel Walker, is seen as a later addition as it has the London hallmark for 1804. It is a semi-precision watch, with a ruby cylinder escapement and a white enamel regulator dial, with a subsidiary dial to indicate the hours and another for subsidiary seconds below. An interesting feature of this watch is the spiral bi-metallic temperature compensator, of a type known as 'the chelsea bun', mounted on a platform pivoted with balance wheel, rack and pinion for mean-time adjustment. Francis Perigal had followed Mudge and others by using compensating devices for temperature changes, but they were a rare feature in watches at that time, found, for example, in watches made by Josiah Emery and Benjamin Vulliamy. There are pictures of this watch and the temperature compensator in the journal of the Antiquarian Horological Society.[75] Formerly in the George Daniels Horological Collection, the watch was sold by Sotheby's on 6 November 2012 for a buyer's price of £21,250.

Watch 3 is in the Victoria and Albert Museum Jewellery Department. The original pair-cases have the mark of Valentine Walker. It is a gold centre-seconds stop-watch, with a cylinder escapement, signed 'Fra Perigal Watch Maker to his MAJESTY London 708'on the backplate and 'Bond Street London 708' on the dust cap. The watch has an attached story: its owner, a Henry Hare Townshend, had been using it to time horses at Enfield race course, when it was stolen by a notorious pickpocket called George Barrington. The thief was caught, tried at the Old Bailey and transported to Australia. The owner had valued the watch at £20 (about £1,120 in today's money).

Watch 4 is the only known example of a Perigal lever watch. The movement of the watch is numbered 1053, a later dust cap being engraved 1079, together with 'Watch Maker to his Majesty'. There is also a later silver case of 55mm, with the hallmark for 1867-8. The watch has gold heart shaped hands and an enamelled dial with the inscription 'PERIGAL BOND STREET'. There is an upper subsidiary dial, dependent on a bi-metallic temperature compensator, with a lower dial for seconds. Watch 4 has been described and illustrated by Cecil Clutton, the owner of the watch in 1957, in articles that he wrote in 1957 and 1978.[76] In Clutton and Daniel's *Watches* (p. 309-10) it is described as a 'very fine watch', the Perigal lever is pictured on page 43 of this book. It is also mentioned, with accompanying pictures, in *The English Watch 1584-1970* (p.302-3) by Terence Camerer Cuss. As the original case is missing it cannot be accurately dated. Clutton and Daniels give its likely date as 1785-6, but it appears from the numbering sequence that the watch was made after 1787. From the appearance of the movement and the dial, Terence Camerer Cuss dates it to 1790.

Francis Perigal's fellow watchmaker to King George III, Thomas Mudge, had revolutionised the accuracy of clocks and watches by his invention of the lever escapement. The Royal Collection at Windsor Castle has a watch known as 'Queen Charlotte's watch' which is considered to be very historically important, as it is thought to be the earliest watch to incorporate Mudge's new invention. From about 1785 a number of London watchmakers, notably Josiah Emery, followed Mudge's example by producing their own experimental lever escapements. Among them was Francis Perigal of Bond Street. Cecil Clutton believed that the Perigal watch has some resemblances to Mudge's watch, speculating that since Francis was a watchmaker to the King, he could well have had opportunities to examine it.[77] As there are also some similarities between the Perigal lever watch and the watches made by Emery, it has been questioned whether this watch, as well as the Perigal watch numbered 460 (Watch 2) could have been supplied from Emery's workshop.[78] Terence Camerer Cuss, however, finds clear differences between the Perigal and Emery lever watches (*The*

English Watch 1585-1970, p.303), pointing out that though Perigal's movement is much the same as that used by Emery for his small sized watches, and the escapement, like Emery's, was most probably made by Richard Pendleton, there are significant differences between them as follows:

> *Unlike Emery, Perigal has employed a plain balance with four arms and eight poising and timing screws. There is a straight bi-metallic strip for regulating the spiral spring, the foot of which is fitted to a rack served by a square in the centre of the regulation index. Again, unlike Emery, Perigal has a conventional cock - the neck with a bald and clearly insane mask - and the lever set at right angles like Thomas Mudge, the fork, however, is mounted on the end of one of the lever arms.*

Watch 5 is a gold quarter-repeating watch of unknown date, engraved 'Fra Perigal Bond Street London 1189'. From the time that Francis Perigal (4) went into partnership with John Duterrau (1) it looks as if his watches were no longer engraved with his individual name, appearing instead as 'Perigal & Duterrau'.

CHAPTER 9

Clock production at Bond Street before Perigal & Duterrau

A MAJORITY OF THE FRANCIS Perigal clocks sold at auction in recent years have the signature of the Perigals of the Royal Exchange, suggesting that the clock production at New Bond Street was lower. From the clocks that can definitely be attributed to Francis Perigal (4) it appears that, unlike the Royal Exchange Perigals, he did not make clocks designed for the Ottoman and Chinese markets. The Perigals of the Royal Exchange had used the services of the trade manufacturer John Thwaites, with Francis of New Bond Street doing likewise, the names of Francis Perigal, Mr. Perigal (or Perigall) appearing frequently in the daybooks from 1788 to 1798. Before 1794, the various Mr. (Francis) Perigals can often be distinguished by 'Bond St.' or 'Royal Exchange' written at the side of the entry. After 1794 until at least 1804, the description 'Royal Exchange' is only attached to 'Messrs Perigal' or 'Messrs Perigal & Son', so it is usually possible to differentiate the entries for the two firms. Many of the entries in the daybooks, for example 'A New Spring Clock', or a 'New 8 day Clock', give very little information about the clocks appearance.

As well as commissions for clocks, Francis Perigal of Bond Street also subcontracted jobs for their repair and maintenance. It is apparent, for example, that his customer, Lord Salisbury owned a turret clock, and a French spring clock, both of which needed attention. On one occasion the journey to Hatfield House appears to have been undertaken by John

Thwaites in person, (though it is possible that the following entry refers to one of his staff):

> **Mr. Perigal Bond St** *The Rt Honble the Lord Salisbury To a Man 1 Day to Oil the Clock & Wind dial & Going down my Self to Set a French Spring Clock agoing* (entry for 8 August 1794)

A voting record for Francis Perigal in 1802 giving his occupation as 'Manufacturing/Watches and Instruments' indicates that he did not make clocks on his premises in New Bond Street. By the end of the 18th century this was not at all unusual, with many reputable makers, including the Royal clockmaker Benjamin Vulliamy, relying on clocks made elsewhere to their detailed designs and specifications.[79] It is likely, however, that Francis Perigal would have supervised the whole process of the manufacture of clocks bearing his name. For example, specifications in the daybooks that two spring clocks were to be fitted into six inch whole arch tortoiseshell cases (20 September 1791) and a round spring clock into a French case (16 June 1793), suggest that Francis had bought the cases and made arrangements for them to be delivered to John Thwaites.

It is apparent that John Thwaites also supplied Francis Perigal with parts of clocks, such as the new spring dial he ordered in October 1794. Thwaites's clock movements were popular with many clockmakers: a Thwaites movement in a six foot Francis Perigal mahogany sold at auction in 1970, was probably just one among the many ordered by Francis Perigal of Bond Street.[80] The firm of Thwaites could also have been involved in a Francis Perigal tavern clock, made circa 1790, a picture of which was used as the frontispiece for *English Dial Clocks* by Ronald E. Rose.[81]

Several entries indicate that Francis Perigal (4) commissioned turret clocks from Thwaites. A commission for a pendulum, ropes and weights (12 January 1795), for example, can possibly be linked to a turret clock dated 1795 attributed to 'Francis Perigal Bond Street'.[82] On at least three occasions the daybooks indicate that Francis had ordered complete turret clocks. One of these, a new small eight day quarter turret clock with gilt figures, was to be taken to Bells Wharf on behalf of Sir Horace Mann (entry for 2 September 1795). Another entry reveals that a new eight day turret clock made on behalf of Mr. Perigal of Bond Street had been installed at Chippenham Park, near Newmarket (entry for 2 September 1793). The many parts of this clock filling six packing cases had taken one man sixteen days to assemble. A further turret clock made by Thwaites for a 'Mr. Fras Perigal' in 1795 had been commissioned by St. Peter's Anglican Church in Jamaica: it is very likely that this was Francis Perigal (4) from Bond Street.[83] The clock is described in the daybooks as a 'new 8 day Quarter Church Clock' with three outside dials and three good musical bells. According to a note at the side of this entry, Thwaites had finished making the clock during the month of December 1795, with the packing cases containing the clock due to be dispatched to the docks on 8 June 1796 (the date of the daybook entry). From there the cases containing the clock were to be shipped to the West Indies on board the *Elizabeth*, which was captained by a Captain Ward.

CHAPTER 10

Markwick, Markham and Perigal

A WATCH MADE BY THE partnership of Markwick, Markham and Perigal with a London hallmark for 1755 indicates that the firm was active in the 1750s, with Brian Loomes giving the dates of the firm as 1751 to 1825.[84] As this firm specialised in watches and clocks for the Turkish market it probably had a connection to 'Markham, Markwick', active behind the Royal Exchange from 1720 – 60, which had a similar business (Britten). It is apparent that the Perigals of the Royal Exchange also made exotic watches and clocks for the Turkish market, so it seems very probable that they were in the partnership of Markwick, Markham & Perigal. Francis Perigal (4) and his brother John would both have been children when this firm began, but it is still possible that the brothers were involved at a later stage of the partnership. This seems unlikely, however, as both of them favoured the conventional London styles as opposed to the more decorative, opulent styles that were designed for the Turkish market. In addition, there is no evidence so far that either of them made clocks or watches with Turkish numerals.

In the British Museum there is a Markwick, Markham and Perigal watch and chatelaine, which was formerly in the Ilbert Collection, the museum commenting in their catalogue that though the watch was legitimately marketed by the firm 'there is every likelihood that the watch was made entirely in Switzerland'.[85] During the first half of the 19th century, as imported watches became increasingly cheaper than those made in Britain, the practice of subcontracting abroad by some London firms became more widespread. These 'pseudo-London' watches were often of inferior quality to genuine London watches.

CHAPTER 11

The Duterrau family of Rose Street, Soho

THE FIRST RECORD OF THE surname Duterr(e)au(x) in England is in 1709, when a Ferdinand Duterraux becomes a godparent at the Huguenot Chapel known as 'Les Grecs'.[86] Since the beginning of the 18th century commercial relations between Switzerland and Britain had been multiplying, with many Swiss males arriving in London.[87] It looks as if Ferdinand was one of them, as on 7 March 1720 a Swiss Friendly Society in London admitted a 'Ferdinand Duterreau' who had been born in Fribourg.[88] Ferdinand may have had an additional motive for leaving Switzerland, his entry revealing that he was a convert to Protestantism. This could have made him unpopular in his home town, where a majority of the population were Catholic.

Ferdinand was a tailor in Soho, where on 14 March 1710 he married Magdalene Gente at the Huguenot Tabernacle Chapel in Milk Alley, giving his age as 'about 33'.[89] Records show the birth of a son, James (or Jacques), who became a watchmaker. Possibly they had a further watchmaking son called Daniel, though no record has been found for his birth. In a Westminster rate book for 1725 Ferdinand rents a property in Rose Street, Soho, the same street where Claude Perigal (1) had his place of business.[90] It is apparent from John Rocque's 1746 map of London that Rose Street, (now known as Manette Street), was a short walk away from the Huguenot Chapel of 'Les Grecs' in Hog Lane. This is the Chapel pictured in a William Hogarth etching called 'Noon', published in 1738,

28

in which Hogarth makes fun of the French mode of dressing: Ferdinand was probably one of the many London tailors making clothes of this type. It has been suggested that Hogarth was picturing actual people, as the Minister on the steps of the Chapel is said to be an excellent likeness of Rev. Thomas Herve, who was the Minister from 1728-55.[91]

Ferdinand died in 1729, giving his occupation in his will (written in French) as a Life Guard of his Majesty King George the Second.[92] As he was over fifty at the time, this was probably some sort of honorary appointment. His widow, Magdalene stayed on in Rose Street after his death, describing herself as a mantua maker of St. Anne Westminster.[93] She appears in a Westminster Burial Transcript for 21 July 1752, as 'Magdalen Duttereau' from Rose Street.

CHAPTER 12

The first generation of Duterrau watchmakers

DANIEL DUTERRAU THE DATES OF his birth and death are unknown, but there is evidence that he was related to Ferdinand and Magdalene. Firstly, it is apparent that he lived in the same street as the widowed Magdalene his name appearing in a list of watchmakers in the parish of St. Anne's in 1749 as 'Daniel Duteroye' from Rose Street, Soho.[94] Secondly, the godparents named in two baptismal records from the Huguenot chapel of La Patente de Soho suggest that Daniel was a relation.[95] All the information available for Daniel shows that he was a watchmaker spending his working life in the parish of St Anne, Soho, records giving several variants of his surname from Duteroye to Duterau. In an indenture dated 1749, for example, a 'Dan Duterau' of St Anne Westminster, watchmaker takes on an apprentice called Thomas Perriman for a fee of £10.[96] Daniel can also be found in Westminster rate books from 1749 to 1753 in Rose Street, Soho. A 1751 rate book shows that one of his neighbours was a Claude Perigal. It is very likely that this was Claude Perigal (2) who had taken over his father's business in 1749.

Daniel's first marriage to Sarah Wheeler was registered at Fleet prison (a Fleet marriage) on 8 October 1738, taking place the same day at 'Lillys the Fleet per Wyatt'.[97] He does not appear to have had much success as a watchmaker, as two of his sons, Louis and Jacques, attended the French Protestant Charity School, set up by some of the richer Huguenots: the school educated children up to the age of fourteen, gave them free board and lodging and paid the fees for their apprenticeships.[98] Neither of Daniel's sons became watchmakers, but a 'Sarah Dutarah', who was probably his daughter, was married on 7 January 1763 to Jean Louis Henchoz, a watchmaker from St Martin in the Fields.[99] Later on, in 1774, a 'Louis Henchoz, formerly of Hog Lane ... watchmaker', appears in the *London Gazette* as a prisoner in the Fleet.[100]

James Duterrau (1) (1713 - ?) The son of Magdelaine and Ferdinand, James was born on 2 November 1713 and baptized at St. Anne Soho.[101] Ferdinand must have had high aspirations for his son, as James attended Winchester College in Hampshire.[102] In the archives of Winchester College there is a record for a pupil called 'James Duttereau' who had been baptised on 15 November 1713 at the Church of St. Anne, Westminster.[103] His record shows that he arrived at the College in 1728 and stayed for two years, leaving at the age of sixteen in 1730. It was customary for scholars at the College to stay until they were eighteen, so is seems probable that James's early departure had been brought about by his father's death in the preceding year. On September 30 1730, James was apprenticed to Francis Perigal (1), his widowed mother, Magdalene paying a fee of £10 (this was before Francis (1) left for the City in 1740).[104] As the canton of Fribourg was not one of the watchmaking areas of Switzerland at the time, it is unlikely that the Duterrau family had any previous history of watchmaking, so it seems plausible that Francis's brother Claude (1) had some role in arranging this apprenticeship. A London marriage licence allegation for 1739 shows that James was intending to marry Mary (or Marie) L'Honorey.[105] Four of their children had horological connections, as in addition to three watchmaking sons, their daughter Mary married Francis Perigal (4), who later became the senior partner of Perigal and Duterrau.

Baillie lists James as London watchmaker pre-1770, but little is known about him. It appears that he started out in Soho, as he was renting property in Chapell Street, Soho in 1744, where he took on an apprentice called J.G.Bevan, for a fee of £17 10s.[106] In 1756, the burial record of his wife Mary shows that they were living in King Street, Soho.[107] By 1769

James had moved to Swallow Street in the district of St. George Hanover Square, where he rented a property for the sum of £8 1s 12d, appearing in the Westminster rate books at the same address until 1775.[108] Two years later James bought a Sun Fire Insurance Policy, which insured a house and its contents at 11, York Row Kennington Common for £400.[109] This house could well have been one of the villas which had been built at Kennington Common in the middle of the 18th century for tradesmen from the City to use as weekend retreats and for eventual retirement.[110] As James was sixty-six at the time, his house was probably his retirement home, but it is possible that he still retained a business at Swallow Street. The only information about the watches made by James comes from an advertisement for a stolen watch in the *Public Advertiser* for 1770, an anonymous owner offering a reward for its return. It is apparent from this advertisement that James made the type of watches that were used by their owners as status symbols.[111]

> Public office, Bow-Street, Jul 13
>
> Stolen a Silver watch, the maker James Duterrau, no 113, with a black Silk String, and two Solid Silver Seals, Impression of one Coat of Arms, three cross Croslets, the other a Head. If offered to be pawned or sold, stop it and the Party and give Notice to Sir John Fielding and you shall receive Two Guineas Reward from the Owner

CHAPTER 13

The second generation: the 3 sons of James Duterrau(1)

BENJAMIN DUTERRAU (1) (1741 – **1822**) He was born in the parish of St. Anne, Soho and baptised at the parish church on 18 February 1741.[112] In 1756, at the age of fifteen, he was apprenticed to Richard Willder, a 'Citizen & Turner of London' for a fee of £20: the 'turns' was an essential tool for watchmakers at this time.[113] As Benjamin became a repeating watch motion maker, it is possible that this was the same Richard Willder who had been apprenticed to Claude Perigal (1) of Rose Street in 1742.[114]

On 8 April 1766, a marriage bond reveals that Benjamin, from 'Westminster St Ann', was about to marry Sarah Culverwell with the consent of her widowed mother.[115] Benjamin's late father–in-law can be found in a list of watchmakers working in St. Anne, Soho in 1749 as 'Nathaniel Culverwell of King Street', his will, dated 1763, naming his two children as Winifred and Sarah.[116] Winifred had married a watchmaker called Jacob Jean Riviere in 1756 with her father as a witness, so both of Nathaniel's daughters married into French speaking watchmaking families.[117] It looks as if Nathaniel was an accomplished workman, as he is listed in a watch daybook as one of the outworkers of the firm of Gray and Vulliamy, just over half of whom had surnames suggesting a French origin.[118] This was a prestigious firm, with Benjamin Gray serving as watchmaker to King George II.[119] Nathaniel's entry in the daybook is as follows: 'cuts balance wheels & fusees, King Street, St Ann's Soho'.

In a petition to the Middlesex Sessions, dated 5 December 1784, a disgruntled apprentice brought a complaint against his master, 'Benjamin Dutereau, repeating watch motion maker' of Rathbone Place, Marylebone. The grounds for Henry Haslip's appeal were as follows:[120]

> *From his having been chiefly employed on Errands by his Master & Mistress and from his own incapacity, he has made very little or no progress in the knowledge of the said Business, although he had served Five years to it .... The said Business being of Mechanical nature and extremely difficult to learn*

The case appears to have been settled amicably, as a later letter to the court reports that as Henry Haslip had left Benjamin's employ the matter was now settled.[121]

Benjamin was one of the many specialised craftsmen involved in watch production at this time, with repeating watches, which could be used to sound the time in the dark, at the upper end of the market. As the motions for these watches required great delicacy and precision to manufacture, their makers could charge at least twice the price of an ordinary watch-motion. Benjamin appears to have made a reasonable living as in 1781 he insures his house at 19, Glanville Street, Rathbone Place, together with the contents including stock, for a total sum of £300.[122] In 1786, a newspaper advertisement for the sale of a house in Rathbone Place 'leaseth to Mr. Dutereau for eight Years', for an annual rent of £50, gives an account of the house where Benjamin was living, describing it as 'Substantial' with 'Offices, Yard & workshops'.[123] The family probably did not have the house to themselves, however, as it was common for London tradesmen who rented a whole house to take in lodgers. There is no evidence to show where Benjamin sold his watch motions, but his brother-in-law, Francis Perigal (4) of Bond Street could well have been one of his customers. By 1814, it is apparent that Benjamin was working for the firm of Perigal & Dutereau at their premises in 8, Poland Street (see later).

Benjamin and Sarah had several children, but their only son to survive to adulthood was Benjamin (2) (1768-1851).[124] He had an artistic talent that would have been useful for a watchmaker, but this was a time when portrait painters were in great demand and Marylebone in particular had large groups of artists.[125] While Benjamin (1) was living at number 37, Newman Street in 1799, for example, the President of the Royal Academy, the American history painter Benjamin West, had a house and studio in the same street at number 14.[126] This particular environment probably influenced his decision to apprentice his son to an etcher, rather than a watchmaker. In 1811 Benjamin (2) married Elizabeth Perigal, who was one of the children of John Perigal, formerly a watchmaker of Coventry Street.[127] His career in England as an etcher and portrait painter was relatively modest: an example of his work, a stipple engraving of a dissenting minister, can be found in the National Portrait Gallery in London.[128] At the age of sixty- four, Benjamin (2) moved to Australia, where he has been credited with making Australia's first etching, as well as its first major history painting, 'The Conciliation'.[129] He is also well-known for his etchings of aborigines, some of which can be found in the British Museum and the British National Portrait Gallery. His father, Benjamin (1) moved to Southampton, where he lived on into his eighties, by which time he had little left to bequeath to his children apart from a treasured 'gold watch & seal', which he valued at £12.[130]

James Duterrau (2) (1745-1793) The second of James (1)'s watchmaking sons was born on 14 November 1745 and baptised as 'Jaques Du Terrau' in the French Huguenot Chapel known as 'La Patente de Soho'.[131] Unlike his two brothers, James (2) did not have any involvement with the firm of Perigal and Duterrau. He must have had some reputation as a watchmaker, however, as he appears among the watch and clockmakers listed in 1782 by the King's clockmaker Benjamin Vulliamy (see endnote 5). His entry is as follows: 'Duterau ... Plumb Tree Street, St. Giles's' (as 'Plumptre Street, St. Giles' in John Rocque's 1746 map of London). In his marriage bond, dated 9 September 1774, he is described as a watchmaker from St. Giles in the Fields.[132] Sometime after 1782 James (2) emigrated to Jamaica, which was seen by many at the time as a place where fortunes could be made.[133] In 1797 *The Columbian Magazine or Monthly Miscellany* of Jamaica (first published in 1796), reported James (2)'s death as follows: 'At Montego Bay .... Mr. James Duterreau Watchmaker'.[134] He appears to have died four years earlier however, as his burial record at the Parish Church of St. James in Jamaica is dated 23 July 1793.[135]

John Duterrau (1) (1755-1814) The youngest of James Duterrau (1)'s watchmaking sons, John was born on 6 June 1755 and baptised at the Huguenot Chapel in Leicester Fields, London as 'Jean Du Terrau' on 22 June, with his parents 'Jaques' and 'Marie' as his godparents.[136] No record of his apprenticeship has been found, but it seems likely that he was apprenticed to his future partner, Francis Perigal (4) of Bond Street. At the age of twenty, very soon after gaining freedom from his apprenticeship, John married (Mary) Elizabeth Cook at St. James the Less in Thorndike Street, Westminster St. James.[137] It was the custom for apprentices to work for their Masters for a further two years after they were freed from their apprenticeships, so John would not have been working for himself at this stage. By 1782, John was living at 17, Clipton Street, Marylebone, where he insured his property, for the sum of £200, including goods 'in Trust'.[138] About sixteen years later he went into partnership with his brother-in-law, Francis Perigal and the firm of Perigal and Duterrau began. John and his son John (2) were certainly the most eminent of the Duterrau watchmakers, both of them obtaining Royal Warrants as tradesmen to the King (see later).

CHAPTER 14

The third and fourth generations of Duterrau watchmakers

JOHN DUTERRAU (2) (1783-1848) John Francis Duterrau, the only son of John (1) and Mary Elizabeth Cook was born in Marylebone in 1783 and baptised at St. Marylebone Church on 25 March 1783.[139] No record has been found for his apprenticeship, but it is likely that he was apprenticed either to his father or his father's partner, his uncle Francis Perigal (4). On 23 January 1812, he married Matilda Webb at the Anglican Church of St. George Hanover Square.[140] According to a family story she was a fine pianist and a pupil of a Mrs. Anderson, who gave lessons to the children of the aristocracy. After the deaths of his father in 1814 and of Francis Perigal in 1817, John Francis inherited the business of Perigal and Duterrau (see later).

Thomas Webb Duterrau (1814-1888) The second son of John Francis Duterrau and Matilda Webb was born at 62, New Bond Street in 1814.[141] No record for his apprenticeship has been found, but he was probably apprenticed to his father. Perhaps his progress as an apprentice was unsatisfactory, as on May 1831, his father wrote to the Colonial Office, to say that he intended to send his son to the new Swan River Colony in Australia as a settler.[142] Founded in 1829, the colony was in the process of being established on the basis of land grants to settlers in exchange for capital investment to improve the land. John was clearly attracted by the idea of free land, as he asks in his letter to be sent the terms of the settlement.

Thomas was only seventeen when he arrived in Australia, so his knowledge of watchmaking could only have been rudimentary, but he gives his occupation as 'watchmaker' in the 1832 census of Western Australia.[143] His business must have been unsuccessful, as in June 1832 he applied for a job in the colony's civil service, stating that he did not make enough money from his watch-repairing business to support himself. By August of 1833, Thomas had opened a store in Perth, selling everything from fencing nails and English clocks to Mordan's Patent Pens.[144] Later that year he was finally allocated his free land, a 'town allotment' in Perth.[145] But it appears that by this time Thomas had gone bankrupt, with all his goods, including his watchmaker's tools, being seized by a bailiff to be sold at public auction.[146]

By November of that year Thomas became disillusioned with Perth, moving on to Hobart in Van Diemens Land, where conditions were easier and he had relatives, his father's first cousin, the Australian artist Benjamin Duterrau (2).[147] Benjamin's house and studio were in Campbell Street and in 1835 Thomas placed an advertisement in a newspaper using his relation's address, as follows:[148]

To the Public

T.W. Duterrau from the firm of PERIGAL & DUTERRAU Watch and Clock makers to His Majesty, New-Bond Street, London, respectfully announces to the gentry and inhabitants of Hobart town and its vicinity, that he will commence business in the above line on Monday next, March the 9th, at No.87, Elizabeth-Street, near Brisbane Street, where he hopes by the strictest attention to merit a share of their patronage.

Campbell-st, March 3, 1835

It is very probable that once again his business did not prosper, as in May 1836 Thomas left Australia to return to England.[149] Apparently by this time he had had more than enough of watchmaking, as after his return to England he moved onto other occupations.

CHAPTER 15

Perigal & Duterrau of New Bond Street and Poland Street

IN ABOUT 1797-8, FRANCIS PERIGAL (4) of 57, New Bond Street acquired a partner, his wife's youngest brother, John Duterrau (1), who was probably already working for him. John was lucky to have had a brother-in-law willing to take him on, as setting up a business on his own, especially in New Bond Street, would have required a substantial sum of money. A watch numbered 1345, with the London hallmark for 1799 indicates that the firm was making watches in that year, the repeating movement of a Perigal and Duterrau watch numbered 1284, showing that they had started at least a year or so earlier.[150] On 20 February 1799, John Duterrau was appointed as one of the watchmakers in ordinary to King George III, the firm placing the first of its many orders for clocks from the trade manufacturer John Thwaites in that same year.[151]

Throughout its existence, the headquarters of Perigal and Duterrau remained at the same house at New Bond Street. The number of the house started out as 57, but in 1807 the street numbering was changed, so number 57 became 62. There is a joint Sun Insurance policy for Francis Perigal and John Duterrau at 57, New Bond Street in 1801, in which the partners insured their house and stock for £700.[153] John was living

The Perigal and Duterrau watch and clockmakers

Figure 1. 60 – 63 New Bond Street in 1838-40 © Guildhall library
(The Perigal & Duterrau shop at number 62 is now
part of Fenwick's department store)

on the premises, as his personal goods are insured for an additional £100 in the same policy. Frederick Perigal mentions in his book that the firm also had premises at Poland Street (p.37), Westminster rate books for 1814 to 1818 showing that Francis Perigal was renting property at 8, Poland Street.[154] It seems probable that these premises were used for the technical part of the business, with workrooms for manufacturing, repairs and maintenance. Witnessing the probate to the will of John Duterrrau (1) in 1814, his older brother, Benjamin (1) describes himself as 'Benjamin Duterrau of 8 Poland Street' indicating that he too had some involvement with the business. The Poland Street premises could also have been used as the Westminster dwelling of Francis Perigal, as according to his burial record, he died at 'Poland Street, Oxford Street, London'.[155]

The original partners of Perigal and Duterrau, Francis Perigal (4) and John Duterrau (1) had both received appointments as watchmakers in ordinary to King George III, but apart from the records of their Royal

Figure 2. A Perigal & Duterrau watchpaper © David Penney
(the paper also gives advice on how to make the watch go slower or faster)

Appointments and the payment to Francis Perigal in 1794 (see earlier) there is no mention of their names in the Royal archives. Traditionally, the role of a Royal watchmaker was to supply watches to be used by the King, either for personal use or as gifts, but so far it has not been possible to find any Royal associations for their watches. This is possibly because watches were considered personal property at the time, so very few of them were inventoried.[156] It is apparent, however, that the partners made the most of their appointments for advertising purposes, the slogan 'Watch makers to his Majesty' appearing on their watches was, according to a descendant of John Francis, also prominently visible in the shop window. Watch papers, used to cushion the inner case in pair-cased watches, were also useful for advertising Royal connections, a watch paper (Figure 2) indicating that the firm had an additional Royal Appointment as 'Watchmaker Extraordinary to the Prince of Wales'.

It was customary for a new King or Queen to appoint or renew appointments for Royal tradesmen soon after the beginning of their reign, so on 5 April 1820, the Lord Chamberlain of the Household, Ingram Hertford requested the gentlemen ushers to 'Swear and Admit' the firm of 'Francis Perigal & John Dutereau' as 'Clock Makers to the King' (George IV).[157] Joint Royal Appointments such as this, to a partnership rather than to an individual, were not common, but in this case the obvious reason is that Francis Perigal had died three years earlier. On 1 September 1830, soon after the succession of William IV, in a similar Royal Warrant, John's son, John (2) (John Francis) was appointed individually as 'Mr. John Duterreau Clockmaker'.[158]

On 24 April 1814, Francis's partner, John Duterrau (1) died at the age of fifty-eight.[159] Three years after John (1)'s death, Francis Perigal also died and was buried at St. Paul, Hammersmith on 1 November 1817, leaving all his estate to his wife, Mary.[160] Francis's widow outlived her husband by fourteen years, living in Hammersmith, where she died in 1831 her will bequeathing 'my Repeating Watch to my nephew John Duterrau of Bond Street'.[161] Francis Perigal and his wife were childless, so it is probable that John Francis had been trained from an early age to take over the business of Perigal and Duterrau. The house at New Bond Street was his home, as well as his place of work since at least 1809, when a 'John Duterraw Junr N62 New Bond Street' insures his property: he must have been a well-dressed young man, as his 'Wearing apparel' is insured for £85 (nearly £3,000 in today's money).[162] In 1817, after the death of Francis Perigal, John Francis inherited the firm. He was only thirty-four at the time, but there is no evidence to show that he took a partner.[163]

By 1820 four children had been born in 62, New Bond Street to John Francis and Matilda.[164] Sometime around this date, like many successful businessmen, he acquired a house in the country, moving his family to Willesden, which at that time was a small village with a green and a pond. It appears that he had given up the annexe at 8, Poland Street, as there are no records to show that he rented property there. According to a family story, on one occasion, when he was driving himself to work from his house in Willesden, John Francis had a narrow escape from a foot-pad. Noticing a poor old lady hobbling along, he had charitably stopped to give her a lift. As she was stepping up into his carriage however, he caught

Figure 3. Portrait of John Francis Duterrau by his cousin Benjamin Duterrau (2) © Jean Wood

a glimpse of sturdy men's boots and trousers emerging from under her petticoats. Realising that the 'old lady' was a man, he dropped his whip and requested the man to be so kind as to pick it up. Luckily he did so, enabling John Francis to make a speedy escape.

Both John Francis and Matilda had strong nonconformist beliefs and soon after arriving in Willesden they joined a group of like-minded pious villagers who had been cast into 'a serious gloom' by 'the Bull-baiting, cockfighting & all kinds of revelling & blasphemy' that took place on Willesden Green on the Sabbath.[165] In 1820, the group bought some land to build a Congregationalist Chapel.[166] The family became keen Congregationalists, with John Francis's wife, Matilda, starting a small school for young boys with a nonconformist outlook, advertising for 'a female of decided piety' to take charge of it.[167] However, the Anglican Church was useful for social contacts with fellow businessmen and customers, so in 1832 John Francis was elected as a vestryman at the Church of St. George Hanover Square, which was close to his business in New Bond Street.[168]

During the period when John Francis Duterrau is listed as a clockmaker to King George IV and to William IV (see earlier), there were several other Royal clock and watchmakers, as both of these Kings were liberal with their appointments: the *Royal Kalendar* from 1821 to 1838 gives the name of chief Royal clockmaker during this period as Benjamin Vulliamy, with the chief Royal watchmaker as Sigismund Rentesch (or Rentzsch).[169] Distinctions between watch and clockmakers were breaking down at the time, for example Sigismund Rentesch is designated as 'Clock and Watchmaker' in a Royal Warrant in 1837, so John could also have had some role as a Royal watchmaker.[170] The job of a Royal clockmaker mainly involved repairing and restoring the clocks in the Royal Collection: winding them was a separate occupation, involving specially employed 'winders'. George IV had collected a large number of highly decorative clocks which have been described as 'works of art first, furniture second and timekeepers a very poor third'.[171] Benjamin Lewis Vulliamy, the last of the famous Vulliamy clockmakers who had been in charge of the clocks in the Royal Collection for many years, spent much time attempting to bring these clocks to perfect accuracy.[172] Unfortunately the contribution of John Francis as a Royal watch and clockmaker is unknown as he appears to have left no impression behind him.

CHAPTER 16

Perigal & Duterrau: watch production

THE VOTING RECORD OF JOHN Duterrau (2) in 1819 giving his occupation as 'Manufacturing/Watches and Instruments' is identical to that of Francis Perigal in 1802.[173] Unlike many other 19th watchmakers who confined themselves to selling repair and maintenance, it appears that the firm did manufacture at least some watches on their premises, though it is apparent that their clocks would have been made elsewhere. The earliest known production number of the firm is 1284, so it is likely that the numbering system followed on from Francis Perigal's previous business (the latest watch known to have been made by Francis Perigal (4) before the beginning of his partnership is numbered 1189). All of the Perigal and Duterrau watches looked at so far are signed 'Watch Makers to his Majesty'.

Appendix B lists twenty-two watches or watch movements made by Perigal and Duterrau from about 1798 until 1838, seventeen of which have their original cases with London hallmarks. Watchmaking at this time involved the assembling of parts made by a large number of independent specialist outworkers, but, apart from the case-maker,

Daniel Willmott, who made at least two of their watch cases, the names of the outworkers supplying Perigal and Duterrau are not known. A Perigal and Duterrau watch circa 1802, numbered 1504 has a quarter repeating duplex movement made by Hawley's of London, indicating that

47

Figure 4. The backplate of a Perigal & Duterrau watch numbered 1597

whole movements from another firm were sometimes used.[174] The movement of a further watch, numbered 2026 (see Figure 5.) appears to have come from abroad, as the back of the dial is scratch signed 'Gael Pas, 12 9 66, Roma'.

From the production numbers of the hallmarked watches it can be seen that the firm produced about 1,080 watches in the period from 1799 to 1838. Some of these watches are relatively commonplace, for example the watch numbered 1993 (pictured on the cover) can be seen as typical of its time and place. But others, such as watch number 1704, a gold quarter-repeating watch with an engraved monogram, or watch number 2026 (pictured in Figure 5.) were more special and would have received personal attention from the partners. These two watches could well have been commissioned by an aristocratic customer for a high price, the seller of the watch numbered 2026 commenting that the cost of the movement alone, cased in gold, would have been enormous when new. This watch is described by David Penney as follows: 'Capped fullplate fusee movement with half-quarter repeating work of best Stogdon-type, elaborate sprung balance- brake operating on the underneath of the flat steel balance, and with finely engraved balance cock and slide plate, the cap with fleur de lys cap markers, often found on top London work. Large brass edge holding the two coiled steel gongs ….. Graham style cylinder escapement with English steel escape'.

Figure 5. Gold quarter repeating Perigal & Duterrau watch (1816) number 2026
©David **Penney**

The Metropolitan Museum of Art in New York has a further unusual gold watch made by Perigal and Duterrau, which had been donated to the museum by J. Pierpont Morgan. The museum gives the production number of the watch as 2401, but it appears as 2041 in the catalogue of his donated watches, dating it to circa 1816.[175] The handsome enamelled case with star ornamentation in white and gold, separated by panels of blue enamel is shown in black and white on the museum's website.

From 1834 to 1836 John Francis had an advertising campaign in London's *Morning Post* to sell gold watches which had been made by the firm in small batches of a like sort. The prevailing style among London watchmakers in the 1830s, influenced by Breguet, was for thinner, lighter watches, with accurate time-keeping becoming increasingly important. It is apparent from the advertisement below and from watch number 2425 in Appendix B that John Francis was trying to keep in step with his competitors by using the latest London style. At a price of nine guineas (about £415 in today's money), these watches were not cheap, but they were not in the luxury range: Horace Walpole in the late 18th century had complained when trying to find a good watch for a friend that he could not find anything respectable under 100 guineas (about £6,000 today).[176]

Morning Post 9 December 1835

> Christmas Presents – Messrs Perigal & Duterrau Manufacturers, beg to announce that they have just finished a fresh Assortment of excellent FLAT GOLD WATCHES of various sizes, jewelled in four holes at 9 guineas each, and which from their neat appearance and correct manner of keeping time will be found most suitable for the above purposes.
>
> To be had of Perigal & Duterrau Makers to the King
> 62, New Bond Street

CHAPTER 17

Perigal & Duterrau: clock production

FRANCIS PERIGAL HAD USED THE services of the trade manufacturer John Thwaites before the start of his partnership and this was to continue. During the period from 1799 to 1808 there are fifty-eight entries for 'Messrs Perigal & Duterrau' in the daybooks of Thwaites and Reed, some for more than one commission, with the last entry, (for cleaning a turret clock) in 1811.[177] The year 1800 is typical of their commissions (see Appendix C). Though the firm no longer appears in the daybooks after 1811, it is apparent that they continued to use Thwaites's products. For example, there is a signed mahogany bracket clock with a repeating mechanism, dated circa 1817, which has an eight day twin fusee movement stamped by Thwaites and Reed.[178] Another example is a small mahogany, brass bound Regency mantel clock dated circa 1820, with an arched case and a Thwaites and Reed movement.[179]

Twenty seven of Perigal and Duterrau's commissions to John Thwaites were for spring clocks with either a five or a seven inch 'Japann'd [painted] Dial Plate Flat Pendulum & Metal hands Gilt'. No mention is made of a case, so arrangements would have been made for them to be cased up and finished elsewhere. It seems likely that some of the spring clocks with seven inch dials were made into small dial clocks: these clocks, which were hung on a wall, were low-priced and generally popular, so it is probable that they were a part of their every-day business.

A later Perigal and Duterrau seven inch dial clock, circa 1835 can be found on page 103 of *English Dial Clocks* by Ronald E. Rose. Several of the other clocks commissioned from Thwaites had refinements, such as the '8 day Clock with 12 in Japann'd dial plate Day of the month' which is mentioned in December 1806. Another entry in the daybooks 'To a Small round Timepiece with 7 in Japann'd dial plate pendulum & Metal hands gilt in brass band ... Brass back' (May 1806) can be matched to a Georgian bracket clock, dated circa 1805, with brass bound case and a seven inch painted dial signed 'Perigal & Duterrau'.[180] A further fifteen of the Perigal and Duterrau commissions to Thwaites were for parts of clocks, such as spring dials attached to boards varying in diameter from twelve to fourteen inches.

In addition to commissions for clocks, Perigal and Duterrau also sub-contracted a total of twelve orders for their maintenance and repair. In May 1803, for example, they asked for the 'Wiping out a Spring Clock name Perigal and Duterrau'. One of their customers was Lord Salisbury, who had already had dealings with Francis Perigal prior to the start of Perigal and Duterrau. An entry for the 25 March 1800 (see Appendix C) shows that a Perigal regulator had been fixed to the wall of Lord Salisbury's house by a man hired from Potters Bar: regulators were precision clocks specially designed to keep accurate time and were commonly used in large households to give a standard time for people to set their clocks and watches by. Further work for Lord Salisbury subcontracted to Thwaites in June 1802 involved the cleaning of an eight day turret clock, the same clock needing new lines in December of that year. In September 1800 a job on a turret clock belonging to another customer required the services of a man working for four days at seven (shillings?) with expenses. The final entry for 'Messrs Perigal & Duterrau' in the daybooks of Thwaites & Reed is for the repair and maintenance of a turret clock in Newgate Street, Hertfordshire in 1811.

George IV, both as Regent and as King, had much influence on the kinds of clocks produced in Britain in the early part of the 19th century, with clocks in the French taste becoming popular in Britain. Recently a Perigal and Duterrau gilt-bronze (ormolu) mantel clock, circa 1810, in a French 'antique' style known as 'Philosophy and Study' was sold at Bonhams. This particular style, with the clock flanked by two seated classical reading figures on a marble plinth and surmounted by a spread eagle was used by several makers, both in France and in England.[181] The Royal Collection, for example, has at least three clocks of this type including one with the signature 'Lepine, Place des Victoires, Paris' on the dial.[182] A similar clock, dated 1798 on the movement springs, is illustrated in an advertisement in the journal of the Antiquarian Horological Society.[183] The Perigal and Duterrau version of the clock has a black and white marble plinth decorated with ribbon tied floral garlands with a central rams head mask. Unlike the similar clocks in the Royal Collection, the two seated figures are both female. A London family called (van) Baetens, made several clocks very similar to the Perigal and Duterrau one. As the Baetens family is described in directories as ormolu manufacturers at 23, Gerard Street and later in King Street, it is likely that they made the ormolu decorations for their own clocks.[184] As some of the elements of the ormolu decorations in the Baeten's clocks appear to be identical to those of the Perigal and Duterrau version, it is likely that the Baeten's family were one of their suppliers.[185]

There is a further Perigal and Duterrau clock in the French style in the National Trust Collection. This is a mantel clock showing many similarities to the one just mentioned. The clock stands on a marble plinth decorated by flower garlands and is flanked by two figures, however, the eagle that surmounted the first clock is replaced by a decorated urn and the two reading nymphs by lions (see Figure 6.)

Figure 6. A Perigal & Duterrau mantel clock in the French style
©The National Trust

CHAPTER 18

The last years of Perigal & Duterrau

By 1845 John Francis had been in charge of Perigal and Duterrau for twenty-eight years, during which time he or his firm had been awarded Royal Appointments by two Kings. During the first decades of the 19th century watch making was going through the stages of becoming a factory system, the many workshops and outworkers that had produced the individual components becoming centralised, so that watches (which were often similar or identical) could be produced in larger numbers. Cheaper foreign watches from countries such as Switzerland, where this system was more advanced, meant that those British firms producing individual hand-crafted watches faced increasing competition. Perigal and Duterrau appear to have suffered from this process: from 1799 to 1816 the firm was producing about forty watches a year on average, but this fell to an annual rate of about seventeen in the period from 1817 to 1838. By 1840 it appears that John Francis was no longer making watches, concentrating instead on retailing and repairing. According to a descendant 'things were not going well' in the last years of the business. Neither of his two sons had shown any interest in taking over: his older son John was a merchant's clerk in Liverpool, while the younger son, Thomas, had given up on watchmaking after his failure in Australia.[186] So in about 1845 John Francis made the decision to sell up. Some of the contents of his shop were auctioned, an advertisement giving a snapshot view of the sort of items that he sold:

The Morning Chronicle Thursday 29 May 1845

> Stock of excellent Gold Watches, Table and Carriage Clocks, Dials, Regulators, Jewellery and Effects of an eminent Watch and Clock Maker, New Bond-street, retiring from business,
>
> MR. PHILLIPS, begs to announce that he will
>
> SELL BY AUCTION, at his Great rooms, 73, New Bond-street on Wednesday June 4 at One precisely, the valuable STOCK, comprising superior gold and silver watches Manufactured in the best manner by Messrs Perigal and Duterreau, also a number of Geneva and French watches, table and carriage clocks, several dials with striking eight and fourteen day movements, a regulator, ormolu and porcelain clocks in the old style, together with a variety of fashionable modern jewellery, including diamond, emerald and ruby rings, gold earings and bracelets, and other objects of decoration .....

On 12 August of the same year, William Payne of 163, New Bond Street advertised his 'Pedometers for Ladies' on sale both at his shop and at 'Messrs Perigal and Duterrau' at 62, New Bond Street.[187] In subsequent advertisements William Payne's 'patent pedometers' are sold at 'Perigal & Co.' of 62, New Bond Street, so the Perigal name had obviously been an important attraction in his decision to purchase John Francis's business.[188] Its manufacturing capabilities could well have been another. Two years later, it appears that John Francis had decided to convert the proceeds of this sale into London property.[189] For the sum of £1,075 he acquired the leasehold of a house at 'Holly Grove, Balham New Clapham London', together with eleven cottages and a piece of land with space for a further ten cottages. His retirement was of a short duration, as he died at his house in Islington on the 22nd of December 1848.[190]

APPENDIX A: THE FRANCIS PERIGAL WATCH AND CLOCKMAKERS

Francis Perigal (1) (1701-67) of St Martin in the Fields, later at 9, Royal Exchange
Apprenticed to Henry Duck (1715)
Partner in the firm of Markwick, Markham and Perigal
Master of the Clockmakers Company in 1756
Apprentices: James Duterrau (1730), Peter Goay (1737), his son Francis Perigal (2), Christopher Beck (1752)
Francis Perigal (2) (1734-1824) of 9, Royal Exchange
Apprenticed to his father Francis Perigal (1) (1748)
Partner in the firm of Markwick, Markham & Perigal
Master of the Clockmakers Company in 1775
Apprentice: his son Francis Perigal (3)
Francis S. Perigal (3) (1764-1843) of 9, Royal Exchange
Apprenticed to his father Francis Perigal (2) (1778)
Master of the Clockmakers Company (as 'Francis S Perigal Junr.') in 1806
Francis Perigal (4) (1742-1817) of St. Giles,
later at New Bond Street and Poland Street (Perigal & Duterrau)
Royal appointment as a watchmaker in ordinary to King George III dated 1 January 1784
Royal Warrant for payment for work as a 'Clockmaker' dated 5 April 1794
Royal Warrant to the firm of Perigal and Duterrau (after Francis's death) as clockmakers to King George IV dated 5 April 1820
Apprentices: John Abraham Goldwin (1765), Solomon Smith (1791)
Francis Perigal (5) of 9, Broad Street, watchmaker (Kent's Directory for 1774)
Francis Perigal (6) of Finsbury Square, watchmaker
A directory for 1805 gives his address as 20, Artillery Place, Finsbury Square (Britten)
Francis Perigal of St. Anne Soho (possibly Francis Perigal (4) before he moved to Bond Street)

Apprenticeship record (TNA, IR/25) 'Fras Perigal' watchmaker of 'St Ann Middlesex', apprentice: Richard Meredith, date of indenture: 28 December 1767, fee: £10

Francis Perigal of Rathbone Place (possibly Francis Perigal (4) before he moved to Bond Street)

Apprenticeship record (TNA, IR 1/26)'Francis Perigal' watchmaker of Rathbone Place, Marylebone, apprentice: Richard Webster, date of indenture 20 June 1770, fee: £40

APPENDIX B: TWENTY-TWO PERIGAL & DUTERRAU WATCHES

Key: CE=Cylinder escapement, DE=Diamond endstone, DP=David Penney's database, G=Gold, H=Hallmarked original case, M=Movement only, MMA=Metropolitan Museum of Art, New York, NH=Without original hallmarked case, R=Repeating, S=Silver

No.	Year		
1284		M, CE, R	Sotheby's, 5.6.1997
1345	1799	H, S, CE(Graham style), consular case	Jones-Horan, 5.10.2013
1444		M, R, CE, repeats quarters by depressing pendant	British Museum (Ilbert)
1465	1802	H	DP
1504		NH, DE, R,(movement from Hawley's London, numbered 1106)	Christie's, 25.9.1996
1528	1803	H, S, whole-hunter case marked W, verge,	British Museum (Ilbert)
1597		M, fusee	Private owner (Figure 4)
1682	1807	H, DE, S, whole-hunter marked DW, fusee,	Antique Watch Store
1704	1807	H, CE, DE, G 18CT, R, open-face, dial with seconds, plunge repeat on 2 gongs, engraved monogram	Christie's, 22.7.1988
1788	1810	H	DP
1927	1813	H	DP

1932	1813	H, CE, G, consular case, casemaker DW	AHS 26/4, p.339
	1814	H, G 18CT, full hunter cylinder	Private owner
1993	1815	H, S, Verge fusee	Private owner (cover picture)
2026	1816	H, CE, G 18CT, R, gold dial with raised pink gold hour numerals, fleur de lys cap markers	Antique Watch Store
2041		G, Gold case enamelled in blue, white & gold	MMA, (Pierpont Morgan Collection)
2068	1817	H	DP
2116	1819	H	DP
2356	1831	H	DP
2400	1834	H	DP
2404		G18CT, open faced, Lepine caliber movement with duplex escapement, case with chased floral decoration	Christie's 6.12.2000
2423	1836	H	DP
2425	1838	H, G, Swiss style duplex escapement, English barrel movement, 18CT gold continental style case, signed hinged gold cuvette, style of watch movement known as élève de Breguet	Jones-Horan, 6.10.2013

APPENDIX C: PERIGAL & DUTERRAU IN THWAITES DAYBOOK (1800)

(The entries in the daybooks of Thwaites and Reed for 'Messrs Perigal & Duterrau' for the year 1800)

25 Jan *To a Spring Clock with 7 in Japann'd Dial Plate Flat Pendulum & Metal Hands Gilt*

25 Mar
Ld
Salisbury *To Cleaning a Regulator Name Perigal Silverd the Dial Plate blued the hands and altered the [?] Case & Packing up & a Man from Potters Bar to put it up*

3 May *To a Spring Dial to a 12 in Board with Brass Hands*

12 Jun *To Cleaning a New Spring Clock & New Line to the Striking part Repair & Paint Dial part*

14 Jun *To a Spring Clock with 5in Japann'd Dial Plate Flat Pendulum & Metal Hands Gilt*

11 Jul *To a Spring Clock with 7 in Japann'd Dial Plate Flat Pendulum & Metal Hands Gilt*

8 Sep   *To a Second Hand 8 day Turrett Clock to Strike the hours on a Bell of a [?] to Show One Outside Dial Plate Hours & Minutes with a New Set of Hour & Minute Dial Works Works to a new Copper Dial Plate of 3-6 with a [?] Moulding Round the edge & Painted black with Gilt figures & Moulding To a Man 4 Days fixing the above at 7 [shillings?] with Expenses*

7 Nov   *To a Japann'd 5 in Dial Plate*

6 Dec   *To a Spring Clock with 7 in Japann'd Dial Plate Flat Pendulum & Metal Hands Gilt*
              To a Spring Clock with 7in Japann'd Plate Flat Pendulum & Metal Hands Gilt

BIBLIOGRAPHY

Atkins, S.E. and Overall, W.H. *Some Account of the Worshipful Company of Clockmakers of the City of London* (privately printed by Blades, East & Blades, 1881)

Baillie, G.H. *Watchmakers and Clockmakers of the World* (Kindle edition)

Berryman, Ian. *A Colony detailed: the first census of Western Australia, 1832* (Perth Creative Research, 1979)   Free online in the catalogue of familysearch.org

Britten, F.J. *Old Clocks & Watches and Their Makers* (Bloomsbury Book 1968, 9th edition)

Camerer Cuss, Terence. *The English Watch 1585-1970*, (Woodbridge: Antique Collectors' Club, 2009)

Clutton, Cecil. & Daniels, George. *Watches* (London: BT Batsford, 1965)

Harcourt-Smith, Simon. *A catalogue of various clocks, watches, automata: and other miscellaneous objects of European workmanship dating from the XVIIth and early XIXth centuries in Palace Museum..* (published Peiping: The Palace Museum, 1933)

Jagger, Cedric. *ROYAL CLOCKS The British Monarchy & its Timekeepers 1300-1900* (Robert Hale, London, 1983)

Loomes, Brian. *Watchmakers & clockmakers of the world: complete 21st century edition* (London NAG press Ltd., 2006)

Moore, Dennis. *British clockmakers & watchmakers apprentice records: 1710-1810* (Mayfield, 2003)

Perigal, Frederick. *Some Account of the Perigal Family*, (published for private circulation, London: Harrison & Sons, 1887)

Rose, Ronald E. *English Dial Clocks* (Antique Collectors' Club, 1978)

Sander, Marie de Gallier. *Traces of our Heritage Vol. 2* (Long Beach California: M.L.Sander, 1989)

John Tallis's LONDON STREET VIEWS 1838-1840 (London Topographical Society, 2nd edition, 2002)

Vulliamy, David G. *The Vulliamy Clockmakers* (The Antiquarian Horological Society, 2002)
Weinreb, Ben. *The London Encyclopedia* (Pan MacMillan, 2008)
White, Jerry. *LONDON in the Eighteenth Century A Great and Monstrous Thing* (The Bodley Head, 2012)

GLOSSARY

BACKPLATE: A plate at the back of a movement

CHATELAINE: A short chain hung from a belt which was used to attach items such as a watch or keys

CLOCKMAKERS' COMPANY: The Worshipful Company of Clockmakers is one of the livery companies based in the City of London

ESCAPEMENT: The regulatory mechanism which allows the power of a watch or clock to be released at a regular rate

HALLMARKS: One element of a watch's hallmark is the date-mark. If the case is original this gives the date of the watch's manufacture

WATCH CASES: The watch is open-faced when there is no cover, hunter-cased if the case gives a solid cover to the dial and pair-cased when there is both an inner case housing the movement as well as an outer protective case

JEWELLED: Precious stones, such as rubies were used to reduce the friction of the movement in the pivot holes

JAPANN'D DIAL: This means that the dial has been painted

MANTEL CLOCKS: These were relatively small clocks produced during the first half of the 19th century, which were designed to stand on a flat surface such as a shelf

MOVEMENT: The engine of the watch, made up of the moving parts apart from the hands

PRODUCTION NUMBERS: Watch movements are usually numbered sequentially, a lower or higher number indicating whether the watch is an earlier or later piece. By correlating these numbers with the dates of the watch's manufacture, it is possible to work out the annual production rate of a watchmaker

REPEATER: A clock or watch that, depending on its sophistication, can repeat the previous hour, quarters and minutes by using a cord or button

ABBREVIATIONS USED IN ENDNOTES

AHS	The Journal of the Antiquarian Horological Society
BM	British Museum
G	Guildhall library in London
HSP	Proceedings of the Huguenot Society of London
HSQS	Huguenot Society of London Quarto Series publications
LMA	London Metropolitan Archives
MMA	Metropolitan Museum of Art, New York
SOG	Society of Genealogists library in London
TNA	The National Archives at Kew, London
WRBT	Westminster rate books transcriptions at findmypast.co.uk

ENDNOTES

Introduction

1. Frederick Perigal, *Some Account of the Perigal Family* (London: Harrison & Sons, 1887)

1. The Perigal watch and clockmakers

2. www.londonlives.org
3. SOG, *St Martin in the Fields Poor Law Records. Settlement Examinations*, Vol.F5028 p.285
4. Britten's *Old Clocks & Watches* has a 'Thomas Perigal, '1812 London, watch'. Clocks made by Thomas Perigal occasionally appear at auctions
5. G, Ref: CLC/C/CD/E/031/MS03961. *A list formed by Mr. Benjamin Vulliamy in the year 1782 of 286 persons carrying on Trade at Clock and Watch Making*

2. Claude Perigal (1&2) at Rose Street, Soho

6. TNA, IR 1/14, Apprenticeship of Stephen La Vigne, Claude was a 'Watchmaker of St Martin in the Fields', fee: £10.
TNA, IR 1/16, Apprenticeship of Richard Willder, Claude was a 'Watchmaker of St Anns Westminster', fee: £31 10s
7. www.jones-horan.com sale on 20 October 2002
8. *London Daily Advertiser* 6 December 1745, p. 3/4
9. HSQS Vol.31, (1928) p.22
10. SOG, *Bank of England Will Extracts*, Book 8, Register 986, Film 64/3, No.22243.
11. WRBT, Folio 30 (Watch rates etc.). The entry for 'Perigal, Claude (2)' in Brian Loomes refers to him as 'London (Rose Street) from 1749'

3. Francis Perigal (1, 2 and 3) at the Royal Exchange

12. HSQS Vol. 29, (1926) p.79 as 'François Perigal'
13. TNA, IR 1/4, date of indenture: 5 October 1715. Henry Duck's trade is not given, but he is described as a 'Citizen & Goldsmith' in two other records, for example the apprenticeship of Tobijah Winne in 1714 (TNA, IR 1/3)
14. TNA, RG 4/ Piece 4549/Folio 4, marriage to Susanne Chartier. Francis (2)'s birth is in *England, Select Births and Christenings 1538-1975*
15. TNA, IR 1/12, Francis Perigal is a watchmaker from 'St Martins Fields' and James is the 'son of Magdelaine Duterrau of Do, Widow', date of indenture: 30 September 1730. The TNA transcript gives the fee as £95, but the same record in Dennis Moore's *British clockmakers & watchmakers apprentice records: 1710-1810* has a more plausible £10
16. TNA, IR 1/15, date of indenture: 20 October 1737
17. *London England, Freedom of the City Admission papers 1681-1925*, as a 'Watchmaker', freedom obtained by redemption (which means he paid for it)
18. *The Worshipful Company of Clockmakers*, online page called 'Clockmaker Masters and their Apprentices'. Francis Perigal (2) was bound to his father on 16 January 1748 and freed on 5 April 1756. Christopher Beck was bound on 18 January 1752, (a Christopher Beck 'app. Francis Perigal' placed an order to Thwaites & Reed on 8 February 1800)
19. HSP, Vol.20 Issue 2, (1958-64) p.174 mentions the three Francis Perigals, father, son and grandson, at the Royal Exchange.

London England, Marriages and Banns, 1754-1921, Francis Perigal (2) married Marie Ogier in the City of London on 8 September 1763.

London England Baptisms Marriages and Burials, 1538-1812, baptism record of St Peter le Poer in the City of London gives the date of birth of their son Francis (3) as 11 June 1764.

Francis (3) was bound to his father, Francis (2) on 6 July 1778 and released on 9 January 1786 (see page mentioned in endnote 18)

20. *The Worshipful Company of Clockmakers*, online page called 'Masters since 1631'
21. TNA, Will of 'Francis Perigal, Clockmaker of Twickenham, Middx'. Date of probate: 27 June 1767, PCC probate no: 11/929/363
22. *The Universal British Directory 1793-1798*, vol.5, p.105, for example, has consecutive entries for 'Perigal, Francis' and 'Perigal Franc. Jun' both from 9, Royal Exchange. Their company is described as 'Clockmakers' and their professions as 'Watchmaker'. In the daybooks of Thwaites & Reed, Ref: MS06788/002 (Guildhall library), they appear as 'Messrs Perigal' or 'Messrs Perigal & Son' from 1793 until at least 1804. These entries usually have 'Royal Exchange' in the margin beside them
23. *London England, Baptisms, Marriages, Burials (1538-1812)*, Francis Perigal (3) was buried at Norwood cemetery on 24 August 1843, Marie de Gallier Sander, *Traces of our Heritage*, p.8, his father, Francis (2) had died in Devon on 8 July 1824,

4. Watch production at 9, Royal Exchange

24. The three watches are as follows:
    (i). No. 17499, dated 1774, AHS (Autumn 1994) Vol.21 Issue 5, p.459
    (ii). No. 19272, dated 1786, Bonhams sale, 13 June 2012
    (iii). No. 20027, dated 1791, AHS (Dec 1969) Vol. 6 Issue 5, p.303
25. Jonathan Betts, AHS (Mar 1996) Vol. 22 Issue 5, p.396
26. Terence Camerer Cuss, *The English Watch 1585-1970*, p.217
27. The watch was sold recently by the Antique Watch Store.com. There is an image of it on the sixth page of the advertisements in AHS (Dec 2014) Vol. 35 Issue 4
28. TNA, IR 1/9, date of indenture, 27 May 1723, fee: £20. Daniel Aveline was Master of the Clockmakers Company in 1771
29. The watch was donated to the Museum by J. Pierpont Morgan. It is mentioned in a catalogue in the Guildhall Library, Ref: 1496: *Catalogue of the Collection of watches belonging to J. Pierpont Morgan*, p.211

30. AHS (Sep 1975) Vol. 9 Issue 4, p. 468. The watch was sold at an auction in 1975
31. Information from David Penney

5. Clock production at 9, Royal Exchange

32. Marie de Gallier Sander, *Traces of our Heritage Vol.2* p.7 (Long Beach, California: M.L.Sander 1989)
33. G, Ref: CLC/B/215/MS06788/002 and 003. The daybooks of Thwaites & Reed have 77 entries for the name Perigal or Perigall between 1784 and 1798, some with the addition of 'Bond Street', others with 'Royal Exchange' in the margin
34. AHS (Dec 1973)Vol. 8 Issue 5, p.466
35. Roger Smith and David Thompson, AHS (Winter 1993) Vol. 21 Issue 2, p.120
36. Roger Smith, AHS (Mar 2008) Vol.30 Issue 5, p. 636
37. Allen H. Weaving, AHS (Summer 1991) Vol.19 Issue 4, p.389
38. Simon Harcourt-Smith, *A catalogue of various clocks, watches, automata…* p.1
39. Sotheby's sale, 7 November 2012, 'A fine silvered, gilt-brass, and blue glass quarter-striking musical automaton table clock …' sold for $542, 500. The clock is signed by 'Francis Perigal Royal Exchange'
40. AHS, (June 2015) Vol. 36 Issue 2, p. 197-8
41. Sotheby's sale, 4 June 2012 of an elephant clock made by Peter Torckler. Sotheby's description of the Peter Torckler clock includes a picture of a version of the clock made by Francis Perigal (figure 3. in their description of the Torckler clock) which is 'now in the Beijing Palace Museum'
42. Christie's sale, 15 Sep 2004. The clock is signed 'Francis Perigal Royal Exchange'

6. John Perigal of Coventry Street

43. TNA, RG4/Piece 4584/Folio 92, *The Register of the Huguenot Chapel at Leicester Fields* as 'I. Perigal Born Jan 28th 1741'. The date of birth of

his future wife, Jane Grellier is written underneath his entry. These two entries were a later addition to the register as they are on a small piece of paper attached to one of the pages

44. TNA, IR 1/20 for 'John Perigall', date of indenture: 5 June 1755, term: 7 years. This record probably belongs to John, as his brother Francis was a watchmaker of St. Giles at the time of his marriage to Mary Duterrau
45. The 'Ring & Pearl' is mentioned in *The London Goldsmiths*, p.219 (Worshipful Company of Goldsmiths 1935, a google book). Also in the *London Gazette*, 10 April 1773, Issue 11343, p.2
46. BM, Banks Collection of trade cards, Ref: D,2.1709
47. *London Gazette*, 15 July 1777, Issue: 11788, p.3
48. LMA, Sun Fire Insurance, MS 11936/264/397781. They are described as 'Goldsmiths, Cutlers, Watchmakers and Toymen' of 12, Coventry Street
49. *Morning Post & Daily Advertiser (London)*, 13 July 1778
50. S.E.Atkins and W.H.Overall, *Some Account of the Worshipful Company of Clockmakers of the City of London* p.184. John and his brother were in the second of the two groups admitted in 1781
51. *London Gazette*, 31 December 1782, Issue:12402, p.2
52. *Newcastle Courant*, 3 July 1784
53. *London Gazette*, 29 June 1799, Issue:15153, p.659
54. BM, the watch was originally in the Ilbert collection. The case has the London hallmark for 1818, but as the partnership of Perigal & Browne was dissolved in 1799 it must have been made at a later date
55. Francis Lambert was appointed silversmith and jeweller to the King on 16 August 1830 (LC 3/68, p.157), LMA, has a Sun Fire Insurance Policy for him at 12, Coventry Street MS 11936/445/814162
56. *John Tallis's London Street Views 1838-1840*, [PART 66] p.172
57. *London Gazette*, 15 August 1797, Issue: 14037, p.791
58. LMA, Sun Fire Insurance Policy, MS 11936/453/ 846772 for Elizabeth Perigal of 34, Warwick Street, dated 30 July 1810
59. LMA, Sun Fire Insurance Policy, MS 11936/459/867669 for Benjamin Duterrau 'of No 9 Buckingham Street Strand, gent', dated 24 February 1812
60. *London, England, Deaths and Burials, 1813-1980*

7. Francis Perigal (4) of Bond Street before Perigal & Duterrau

61. This is the date given in Frederick Perigal's book. It fits with the age given at Francis's burial on 1 November 1817 in *England, Select Deaths and Burials, 1538-1991*
62. Westminster Marriage Transcripts and images from findmypast.co.uk
63. TNA, IR 1/24, date of indenture: 22 Oct 1765
64. WRBT, Folio 5, Paving Rate Collector's Book, 1778-1782
65. LMA, Sun Fire Insurance policy, MS 11936/271/408821
66. Ben Weinreb, *The London Encyclopedia*, p.81. According to Jerry White, *LONDON in the Eighteenth Century*, p. 209, Bond Street had become established as a shopping street in the early years of the 18th century
67. TNA, IR 1/35, date of indenture: 8 Dec 1791, term: 7 years
68. Bailey's London Directory for 1790, for example, with Francis trading from 57, New Bond Street
69. TNA, LC 5/26, p.39, the page is headed 'Tradesmans Bills and for Extraordinaries'
70. David Vulliamy, *The Vulliamy Clockmakers*, p. 18, the Royal appointment for Benjamin Vulliamy in 1773 came with a salary of £150 per annum
71. Cecil Clutton, AHS, (March 1972), Vol.7 Issue 6, p.150
72. G, MS06788/001 and 002
73. The entry for 30 September 1785 shows that work was done for 'Lord Salisbury Hatfield House', but it does not specify which 'Mr. Perigall' had commissioned it. However, the other five entries mentioning Lord Salisbury all indicate that it was Mr. (Francis) Perigal from Bond Street

8. Watch production at Bond Street before Perigal & Duterrau

74. Watch 1: Cogs and Pieces sale
    Watch 2: Sotheby's sale, 6 November 2012,

Watch 3: Victoria & Albert Museum, museum number 1832-1869
Watch 4: Perigal's lever escapement watch is mentioned in several books and articles
Watch 5: jones-horan.com sale, 15 October 2011

75. AHS (Dec 1978), Vol.11 Issue 2, p.96. The picture of the dial as it was in 1978 shows that the hands had been changed sometime before it was sold at Sotheby's
76. AHS (Dec 1957), Vol. 2 Issue 5, p.86-88 and AHS (Winter 1978) Vol. 11 Issue 2 p.95
77. Cecil Clutton and George Daniels, *Watches*, p.143. See also Cedric Jagger, *Royal Clocks*, Figs. 145-7
78. Paul Tuck, AHS (Jun 1997) Vol.23 Issue 4, p.89

9. Clock production at Bond Street before Perigal & Duterrau

79. David G. Vulliamy, *The Vulliamy Clockmakers*, p.34. Only 'exceptional and unusual items' were still made on their premises by the end of the 18th century
80. AHS (Dec 1985) Vol.15 Issue 6, p.102 for 'Fra Perigal, Bond Street', Phillips auction
81. Ronald E. Rose, *English Dial Clocks*, frontispiece and p.17, also pictured in AHS, (Sep 1970) Vol. 6 Issue 8, p.75

10. Markwick, Markham & Perigal

82. AHS (Jun 1969), Vol. 6 Issue 3, p. 46. Auction sale of a 'rare turret clock and bell, two trains with ropes and massive weights, posted frame, 17 in by 20 in wide (£90).'
83. www.visitjamaica.com/falmouth-heritage-walks According to this website the clock was commissioned by Francis Perigal of Bond Street. The clock was commissioned in 1795, a time when the Perigals of the Royal Exchange appear in the daybooks only as a father and son partnership

84. Markwick, Markham & Perigal watch no:13783, Bonhams sale 14 Sep 2010, London hallmark for 1755
85. BM, number 1958,1201.42, the number on the movement is 12959
86. TNA, RG4/Piece/4644/Folio 19

11. The Duterrau family of Rose Street, Soho

87. Bibliothèque numérique RERO DOC, *La Fédération Horlogère Suisse*, no. 13 p. 59 mentions the increasingly important commercial relationships between England and Switzerland during the eighteenth century, with bankers from Berne and Geneva becoming established in London. Many Swiss men came to London, but most of them did not stay permanently
88. *La Société des Suisses* établie *à Londres*, (in the records of the Swiss Church in London), entry number: 131 on folio 73L.
   Under place of birth his entry reads 'de Fribourg, Proselyte'
89. HSQS, Vol.29, (1926) p.14, Ferdinand's marriage. His marriage bond allegation is in LMA, MS 10091/46. According to this document they were intending to get married at the Church of St Martin in the Fields. He gives his parish as St. Anne, Westminster
90. WRBT, as 'Detairo'
91. HSP, Vol.11 (1915-7) Issue 1, p.77

12. The first generation of Duterrau watchmakers

92. LMA, Call number: AM/PW1729/092, *London, England Wills and Probate, 1507-1858*, Archdeaconry Court of Middlesex
93. TNA, IR 1/13, 'Magdalene Du Terreau' was the master.
   WRBT (1634-1753): in the 1730 transcript Magdalene is described as 'Widow Detarroe', the 1748 rate books have both 'Claud Perigall' and 'Mrs. Detrow'
94. AHS (Mar 1954) Vol.1 Issue 2, p.21

95. HSQS Vol 45 (1956), Magdalene is the godmother of Daniel's daughter, Anne (p.40). In the same volume (p.39) Daniel is the godfather of Mary Duterrau the daughter of James Duterrau (1): this is the Mary who later married Francis Perigal of Bond Street. Mary's birth date is given as 8 January 1746 (as the Julian calendar was still in operation this was actually 1747)
96. TNA, IR/18, date of indenture: 16 May 1749
97. TNA, RG7/Piece 165/Folio 48, *Marriages from Walter Wyatt's Register*
98. HSP, Vol. 4 Issue: 4 (1917-23) *Records of the French Protestant School. The Names of Boys registered for Admission.*

    Louis, born 1749, is on page 378. Jacques, born 19 April 1745, is on page 380 as Jacques Du Ferreau, son of Daniel and Sara. A footnote in HSP Vol. 12 Issue: 2, p.14 corrects his surname to 'Du Terreau'. There was another James Duterrau born later the same year - James (2), the son of James (1) was born on 14 November (also baptised as Jacques)
99. Westminster marriages at findmypast.co.uk. She signs her name as 'Sarah Dutarah', but the witnesses to the marriage both sign as 'Mary Duterrau'.

    TNA, IR 1/25 has a Jean Louis Henchoz, a watchmaker from St Martin in the Fields, taking an apprentice in 1766 for a fee of £8
100. *London Gazette*, 25 June 1774, Issue Number: 11469, p.7
101. *England, Select Births & Christenings 1538-1975*. As 'Duteron' (no first name), his father is named as 'Ferdinand Duteron' and his mother as 'Magdalen', with the birth date given as 2 November 1713 and the baptism date as November 1713
102. *Winchester Long Rolls*, Author: Winchester College, published in 1904, p.14. James's name appears as 'Dutereau'
103. Personal communication from the archivist at Winchester College. James was also listed in the rolls in 1726 and 1727, though not in the list of pupils at the school, indicating that he had unsuccessfully tried for election as a scholar in both of those years

104. The details of James's apprenticeship are in endnote 15
105. LMA MS10091/7, *London and Surrey, England Marriage Bonds and Allegations 1597-1921*, dated 2 August 1739. According to this bond, they were planning to marry at the French Chapel at West Street, in Lincolns Inn, Soho. However, they do not appear in the marriage records from 1739-40 for this church
106. TNA, IR 1/17, indexed as 'James Duttercan', date of indenture: 14 Dec 1743
107. WRBT, burial of Mary Duterrau, 21 October 1756
108. *London, England, Land Tax Records, 1692-1932* as 'James Duterreay'. He can also be found at Swallow Street in Westminster rate books from 1769 to 1775
109. LMA, Sun Fire Insurance Policy, MS 11936/277/416677, dated 29 July 1797. Total of £400 (household goods £250, wearing apparel £70, plate £30, glass and china £50)
110. Jerry White, *LONDON in the eighteenth century*, p.34
111. *Public Advertiser*, 1 August 1770, p.2 col.4. This paper campaigned for victims of theft to bring information to Bow Street, where Sir John Fielding was building up a register of criminal records (Jerry White, *LONDON in the eighteenth century*, p.435)

13. The second generation: the three sons of James Duterrau (1)

112. *England Select Births & Christenings 1538-1975*
113. TNA, IR 1/20, date of indenture: 3 Apr 1756, term: 7 years, place: London
114. See information on Claude Perigal (1)
115. *London and Surrey, England, Marriage Bonds and Allegations, 1597-1921*
116. AHS (1954) Vol.1 Issue 2, p.21, *Watch and Clockmakers in Westminster – 1749* Will of 'Nathaniel Culverwell, Watchmaker of Saint Ann Westminster', probate date: 11 October 1763, PCC probate number: 11/892/361

117. *London, England, Marriages & Banns, 1754-1921*, the marriage was on 27 November 1756 at St. Marylebone Church
118. Roger Smith, AHS (2006), Vol.29 Issue 3, p.355. The article warns that appearing on this list should not be taken as proof that they worked for the firm, though it is thought that most of them did
119. TNA, LC 3/65, p.136
120. LMA, MJ/SP/1774/12/077
121. LMA, MJ/SP/1775/01/076
122. LMA, Sun Fire Insurance, MS11936/293/444424 for 'Benjamin Duterreau, watchmaker' at 19, Glanville Street, Rathbone Place
123. *Morning post & daily advertiser*, Saturday 9 October 1786 p.4
124. *English Select Births and Christenings 1538-1975*, 2 March 1768
125. Jerry White, *LONDON in the Eighteenth Century*, p.282 mentions the 'strong clusters' of artists in Marylebone at a time when 'artists were in great demand'
126. LMA, Sun Fire Insurance, MS11936/413/684681 for 'Benjamin Duterrau No 37 Newman Street Watchmaker': £140 for the house, which belonged to 'Aris a grocer', £80 for wearing apparel, £80 for 'Utensils, Stock & Goods in Trust. Jerry White mentions Benjamin West 'the great American history painter ' on page 286
127. *England Select Marriages 1538-1973*, 7 May 1800 at the church of St Martin in the Fields
128. The National Portrait Gallery, Ref: NDG D 11024, a portrait of Joseph Towers (1737-1799), biographer and dissenting minister, stipple engraving 'probably by Benjamin Duterreau'
129. *Magazine of Australian & International Portraiture*, June-August 2009, article by Michael Desmond
130. Will of 'Benjamin Duterrau of Southampton, Hampshire', date of probate: 15 May 1822, PCC probate number: 11/1656/344. Benjamin is described in the will as a watchmaker 'formerly of Poland Street'
131. HSQS, Vol. 45, p.39. He was baptised on 4 December 1745, with his parents as his godparents

132. LMA, Call number: DW/MP/084/066, for 'James Dutteran', Diocese of Winchester, Archdeaconry of Surrey
133. David Dobson, *Scots in Jamaica, 1655-1855*, (published online in 2011), mentions that Jamaica in the mid 18th century was seen by many as a land of opportunity, attracting many professionals, including skilled tradesmen
134. www.jamaicanfamilysearch.com
135. www.jamaicanfamilysearch.com, as follows: BOO55, St. James Parish Register I & II, 1770-1825, I, p.366, for 'James Dutereau'
136. HSQS, Vol. 29, p.171
137. Westminster marriage transcripts, (findmypast.co.uk), date: 13 August 1775. Both John and his wife came from the Parish of St. James. Elizabeth's first name is given as Mary in the birth records of their three children
138. LMA, Sun Fire Insurance Record: MS11936/297/451438

14. The third and fourth generations of Duterrau watchmakers

139. *London, England, Baptisms, Marriages and Burials, 1538-1812*, indexed as 'John Francis Duttereau'
140. London, England, Baptisms, Marriages and Burials, 1538-1812
141. *Westminster Baptisms*, born 28 Sep 1814, baptised 2 May 1816, St George Hanover Square
142. TNA, CO 18/8 p.59
143. John Berryman, *A colony detailed: the first census of Western Australia*, p.47. All the following information on Thomas Duterrau in Australia, apart from the newspaper advertisements, comes from pages 47 and 114 in this book
144. *The Perth Gazette and Western Australian Journal*, Saturday, 31 August 1833
145. *The Perth Gazette and Western Australian Journal*, Saturday 28 December 1833
146. *The Perth Gazette and Western Australian Journal*, Saturday 1 February 1834

147. *Colonial Times (Hobart)* 25 November 1834 reports that a 'Mr. Dutereau' had arrived in Hobart on the schooner *Eagle* from Swan River on 2 November
148. *Colonial Times (Hobart)*, Tuesday 3 March 1835
149. *The Hobart Town Courier*, Friday 6 May 1836

15. Perigal & Duterrau of New Bond Street & Poland Street

150. Watch no. 1345, jones-horan sale on 5 October 2013.
     Watch no. 1284 (repeating movement only) Sotheby's sale on 5 Jun 1997
151. TNA, LC 3/68, p.49. John's Royal Appointment is in the *Database of Court Officers 1660-1837*, a free online database indexed by R.O. Bucholz G, Daybooks of Thwaites & Reed, MS06788/003
152. Figure 1 is a copy of an original drawing by John Tallis at the Guildhall Library. There is a later version of this drawing in *John Tallis's London Street Views 1838-1840*, p.59 [PART 9]. The index in this book gives the name of the shop at 62, New Bond Street as 'Perigal and Duterreau, Watch and Clock Makers'
153. LMA, Sun Fire Insurance policy at 57, New Bond Street MS11936/419/12549 for 'Francis Perigal and John Duterrau, 57, New Bond Street watchmakers'
154. WRBT, the rate book transcripts for 1814 and 1815 do not give the number of the house
155. *London, England, Deaths & Burials 1813-1980*, Bishop's Transcript, burial in Hammersmith, date: 1 November 1817
156. Information from Sally Goodsir of the Royal Collection Trust
157. TNA, LC 3/69, p.8
158. TNA, LC 3/69, p.159
159. *London, England, Deaths and Burials, 1813-1980*, burial on 29 April 1814 of John Duterrau at St. Mary, Paddington Green
160. Will of 'Francis Perigal, watchmaker of New Bond Street, Middlesex', date of probate: 31 January 1818, PCC probate no:11/1600/491

161. Will of 'Mary Perigal otherwise Perrigal, Widow of Hammersmith' date of probate: 10 October 1831, PCC probate no. 11/1791A/374
162. LMA, Sun Fire Insurance, MS11936/448/825834, for 16 January 1809
163. My grandmother remembered being told that the business passed into his hands entirely
164. *Westminster Baptisms*, his daughter, Matilda Sarah Duterrau, for example, was born on 30 Dec 1815 and baptised on 18 May 1816 at St. George Hanover Square
165. LMA, N/C/59, an account of the setting up of the Willesden Congregational Chapel by a relation of one of its founders
166. LMA, ACC/0958/5. This document names one of the founders of the Chapel as 'John Duterrau of New Bond street, Clock and Watch maker'
167. *The Patriot*, 3 August 1837, p.1
168. *London Morning Chronicle*, 30 May 1832, one of the successful candidates was '1491 Duterrau, Mr. 62, New Bond-Street'
169. Cedric Jagger, *Royal Clocks*, p.312-4. These included Royal appointments specifying Edinburgh, Dublin, Brighton and Windsor
170. TNA, LC 3/69 p.150
171. Cedric Jagger, *Royal Clocks*, p.120
172. David G. Vulliamy, *The Vulliamy Clockmakers*, p.32

16. Perigal & Duterrau: watch production

173. www.locatinglondon.org, for 'PERIGAL, Francis, Year: 1802' and 'DUTERRAN, John, Year: 1819'. The address for both of them is 'Bond Street'
174. Christie's sale, 25 September 1996. A Thomas Hawley was made a watchmaker in ordinary to King George IV in 1820 (LC 3/69, p.9)
175. G, Store 1496 *Catalogue of the collection of watches: the property of J. Pierpont Morgan*, John Pierpont Morgan (1837-1913), Mackie, Lilian, Williamson, George Charles, (priv. print. Chiswick Press, 1912)

176. Jerry White, *LONDON in the Eighteenth Century*, p.216

17. Perigal & Duterrau: clock production

177. G, the daybooks of Thwaites and Reed, MS06788/003 and 004
178. Regency mahogany and brass inlaid bracket clock with repeat, front brass plate stamped T &R and 5930, 60cm tall, Woolley and Wallis sale 19 April 2011
179. Regency mantel clock circa 1820, inside case numbered 1836, 29 cm tall, stamped 4835 on the inside of the case. Christie's sale 14 July 2014
180. Flame mahogany, break-arch bracket clock, double fusee 8 day striking movement, 7 in dial, regulating pendulum, anchor escapement, Olde Times sale
181. The Perigal and Duterrau version of this clock was sold at Bonhams on 17 June 2014
182. Cedric Jagger, *Royal Clocks*, p.154. This is the address of Jean-Antoine Lépine, the inventor of the calibre movement that bears his name
183. AHS (Jun 1997) Vol.23 Issue 4. The clock is pictured on the first page of the advertisements
184. *The Post Office Annual Directory* for 1814, for example, lists 'Baetens & Co.' (sometimes listed as 'van Baetens') of 23, Gerard Street as 'bronze or-mulu manufacturers'. The books of the seated maidens in a Baetens clock (Bonham's sale 14 December 2010) are inscribed 'V.B.Fecit, no 63, King St London'
185. The decorations on the plinth, as well as the classical maidens of a Baetens clock advertised by Asprey's in *The Connoisseur* of September 1976 are identical to those on the Perigal and Duterrau clock

18. The Last years of Perigal & Duterrau

186. John's occupation is given in the General Register Office birth certificate of his son, Louis Henry French Du Terreaux on 12 Sep 1840

(both John and his brother Thomas changed the spelling of their surname to Du Terreaux)
187. *Morning Post 12 August 1845, p.1 col.1*
188. *Morning Post 19 Feb 1846, p.9*
189. My third-cousin, Jean Wood has a copy of the original documents concerned with the purchase of the land and property
190. General Register Office, death certificate

Printed in Great Britain
by Amazon